J. Marshall Crawford

Mosby and his Men

A Record of the Adventures of that renowned Partisan Ranger, John S. Mosby

J. Marshall Crawford

Mosby and his Men
A Record of the Adventures of that renowned Partisan Ranger, John S. Mosby

ISBN/EAN: 9783337176518

Printed in Europe, USA, Canada, Australia, Japan

Cover: Foto ©ninafisch / pixelio.de

More available books at **www.hansebooks.com**

JOHN S. MOSBY

MOSBY AND HIS MEN:

A RECORD OF THE ADVENTURES OF THAT RENOWNED PARTISAN RANGER,

JOHN S. MOSBY,

[COLONEL C. S. A.]

Including the exploits of Smith, Chapman, Richards, Montjoy, Turner, Russell, Glasscock, and the men under them.

BY

J. MARSHALL CRAWFORD

OF COMPANY B.

NEW YORK:
G. W. CARLETON & CO., Publishers.
LONDON: S. LOW, SON & CO.
MDCCCLXVII.

Entered according to Act of Congress, in the year 1867, by
GEO. W. CARLETON, & CO.,
In the Clerk's Office of the District Court for the Southern District of New York.

J. E. FARWELL & CO.,
Stereotypers and Printers,
27 Congress St., Boston.

TO

THE SOLDIERS

OF THE

43d Battalion of Virginia Cavalry,

I RESPECTFULLY DEDICATE

THIS BOOK,

AS A MARK OF MY ESTEEM.

It is a record of personal recollections of your achievements during the late war. Although not so elaborate a work as I could wish to offer you, yet it is a faithful and correct narrative written from memoranda made of events as they occurred, by one of your comrades, who, from the earliest organization of our command, shared with you your hardships and defeats, until the disbanding of the command at Salem.

Although not so voluminous as it might be, yet this work contains an account of all the important movements of the command.

Some of my Northern readers may consider the work a little too "rebellious," and may charge me with presenting the acts of some of their men in colors too dark. But let them travel through the country their armies have traversed, and they will see too many proofs of the truthfulness of the picture. The once happy homes and smiling faces no longer greet the stranger. The blooming fields, the orange-groves and extensive flower-gardens, no longer cheer the tourist or protect the wearied traveller from the burning sun of the South. The Southern flag no longer floats over its brave defenders; but the scenes and trials of the Southern people during this contest cannot be forgotten by those who saw and felt them. The history of the struggle will be written hereafter, when passion shall have cooled, and the historian shall be a philosopher, and not a fanatic. Then many things shall assume a different appearance from that which they now present; but no historian will ever say that the 43d Battalion of Virginia Cavalry proved recreant to their duty.

To Colonel Mosby's father and mother, I return my most sincere thanks for assistance rendered me when I commenced my enterprise.

To George Palmer, Esq., of Richmond, Va., I tender my obligations for similar favors rendered in 1865; while Major Richards, Captains Glasscock and Richards, and other members of the command, will please accept my grateful remembrance for the encouragement given me in my feeble efforts to narrate the deeds of heroism done by our command.

J. M. C.

LOUISVILLE, KY.

CONTENTS.

CHAPTER I.
THE SITUATION — BOMBARDMENT OF FORT SUMTER — PRESIDENT LINCOLN'S PROCLAMATION — RIOT IN BALTIMORE — PERFIDY OF THE GOVERNOR OF MARYLAND — TREATMENT OF THE CITIZENS OF BALTIMORE, ... 11

CHAPTER II.
EXCITEMENT IN WASHINGTON — GOVERNMENT CLERKS CALLED UPON TO ENROLL THEMSELVES — AUTHOR LEAVES WASHINGTON — ARRIVES IN MONTGOMERY — ENTHUSIASM OF THE SOUTHERN PEOPLE — SEAT OF GOVERNMENT REMOVED TO RICHMOND, ... 23

CHAPTER III.
PREPARATIONS FOR WAR IN RICHMOND — BEAUREGARD ARRIVES IN RICHMOND — BUTLER MARCHES TO BETHEL AND BACK — BATTLE OF MANASSAS — DISORDERLY RETREAT OF THE YANKEES — REJOICINGS IN RICHMOND, ... 35

CHAPTER IV.
MCCLELLAN'S ANACONDA — ACCOUNT OF MOSBY'S FAMILY AND EARLY LIFE — MOSBY RESPONDS TO THE CALL OF THE GOVERNOR — BATTLE OF SEVEN PINES — MOSBY PENETRATES THE LINES OF THE ENEMY, AND LEARNS MCCLELLAN'S PLANS — BOLD ESCAPE, ... 46

CHAPTER V.
MOSBY'S RAID ROUND THE ENEMY — IS TAKEN PRISONER — BATTLE OF HARRISON'S LANDING — STONEWALL JACKSON'S VISIT TO RICHMOND — MOSBY EXCHANGED — POPE DEFEATED — HOOKER DEFEATED, ... 54

CHAPTER VI.
MOSBY RECEIVES HIS COMMISSION AS CAPTAIN — KILPATRICK AND DAHLGREN — ALARM IN RICHMOND — HOOKER'S DEFEAT — DEATH OF STONEWALL JACKSON — SORROW OF THE SOUTHERN PEOPLE, ... 63

CHAPTER VII.
LEE'S INVASION OF THE NORTH — MOSBY'S CAPTURE OF GENERAL STOUGHTON — THE CONFEDERATE SOLDIER FROM NEW ENGLAND — GENERAL ORDER BY GENERAL STUART — CAPTURE OF WAGONS, ETC. — REMARKABLE ESCAPE OF MOSBY, 71

CHAPTER VIII.
LEE'S MARCH INTO PENNSYLVANIA — THE CONDUCT OF HIS ARMY CONTRASTED WITH THAT OF THE FEDERALS — BATTLE OF GETTYSBURG — MOSBY ACTIVE — EXTRACT FROM A MONROE, OHIO, PAPER, ... 82

CHAPTER IX.

FEELING OF THE SOUTHERN PEOPLE — RECRUITING — THE WRITER JOINS MOSBY — ADVENTURES ON THE WAY — MOSBY'S APPEARANCE, ... 94

CHAPTER X.

MOSBY GAINS IMPORTANT INTELLIGENCE FOR GENERAL LEE — APPEARANCE OF THE BATTLE-FIELD AT MANASSAS — CHARGE UPON A PARTY OF THE ENEMY — CONDUCT OF A NEW RECRUIT — CAPTURE OF WAGONS, ETC. — A VERY SOFT THING IS FOUND TO BE TOO HARD, ... 105

CHAPTER XI.

AFFAIR WITH A DETACHMENT OF CAVALRY — CAPTURE OF A WAGON-TRAIN — ORGANIZATION OF ANOTHER COMPANY — FEASTING — ATTACK UPON THE CAMP AT WARRENTON — PRISONERS, ETC., TAKEN, ... 117

CHAPTER XII.

CAPTURE OF TWO CORRESPONDENTS OF THE "NEW YORK HERALD" — EXPEDITION TO CAPTURE GOVERNOR PIERPONT — RAID TO BEALTON STATION, ETC. . . 127

CHAPTER XIII.

MOSBY CAPTURES ONE HUNDRED AND TWENTY MULES AND TEN HORSES FROM A WAGON-TRAIN, BURNING FORTY WAGONS — YANKEYS CAPTURED — BOLD EXPLOIT OF MONTJOY, ... 134

CHAPTER XIV.

AFFAIR WITH COLONEL COLE'S CAVALRY — SIXTEEN OUT OF EIGHTY "LEFT TO TELL THE TALE" — CAPTURE OF HORSES, ETC. — EXCESSIVE COLD — SPLENDID SCENE 140

CHAPTER XV.

CAPTURE BY LIEUTENANT TURNER AND HIS MEN — MEN FROZEN — CAPTAIN STRINGFELLOW — DARING EXPLOIT, ... 148

CHAPTER XVI.

PLAY AT ALEXANDRIA, ENTITLED, "THE GUERILLA" — MEETING AT UPPERVILLE EXPEDITION — PLAN OF CAPTURE — FAILURE OF PLAN — LOSS OF SMITH, TURNER, PAXON, COLSTON, ETC., ... 154

CHAPTER XVII.

DESPONDENCY OF MOSBY AND HIS MEN AFTER THE HARPER'S FERRY DISASTER — CAPTURE OF A SUTLER'S WAGON, AND A CORRESPONDENT OF THE "NEW YORK TRIBUNE" — CAPTURE OF A PICKET BY MONTJOY — ORDER OF GENERAL PLEASANTON, ... 167

CHAPTER XVIII.

JOHN CORNWALL'S REVENGE — TWENTY-FIVE OF OUR MEN CAPTURED — CAPTAIN CHAPMAN'S ATTEMPT TO RESCUE THEM — THE ENEMY TAKE HORSES, CHICKENS, ETC. — MOSBY'S MEN SLEEP IN CAVES, ETC. 172

CHAPTER XIX.

AFFAIR AT DRAINSVILLE — ATTACK UPON COLONEL COLE — "PRIVATE" OPERATIONS — MOSBY LIES IN WAIT FOR A DETACHMENT — EVACUATION OF WARRENTON — RAID INTO THE VALLEY, ... 181

CONTENTS.

CHAPTER XX.
EXPLOIT OF LIEUTENANT CHAPMAN — VISIT OF A GERMAN BARON — "GOING THROUGH" — OUR "TACTICS" — NARROW ESCAPE — CAPTURES OF WAGONS, ETC., . 190

CHAPTER XXI.
CAPTURE OF A VIDETTE BY JOHN RUSSELL — DISAPPOINTMENTS — VARIOUS OPERATIONS — BOB WALKER, LIKE CHARLES SECOND, ESCAPES BY CLIMBING A TREE — KEYES'S CAVALRY, ... 197

CHAPTER XXII.
CHARGE OF BUSHWHACKING — A DARKEY BUSHWHACKER — UNION CITIZENS OF WATERFORD — A "TRAP" — ARTILLERY — SURRENDER AT DUFFIELD — LIEUTENANT NELSON, ... 203

CHAPTER XXIII.
GOING INTO MARYLAND — STRICT ORDER IN MARCHING — SKIRMISHING ACROSS THE POTOMAC — A DINING PARTY INTERRUPTED — THE EAGLE CAKE — "GOING THROUGH" — YOUNG MARTIN, ... 210

CHAPTER XXIV.
MAJOR FORBES "COMES FOR WOOL AND GOES HOME SHORN" — MOSBY'S LIFE SAVED BY TOM RICHARDS — SOLDIERLY BEARING OF MAJOR FORBES, . . 224

CHAPTER XXV.
STRINGENT ORDERS AGAINST PLUNDERING — EARLY'S APPROACH TO WASHINGTON — CONSTERNATION THERE — EXPLOITS OF CHAPMAN — ORGANIZATION OF COMPANY E — THE POTOMAC RECROSSED — A BRILLIANT FEAT, . . . 230

CHAPTER XXVI.
CAPTURES AT BERRYVILLE — NEW UNIFORMS — LIEUTENANT GLASSCOCK CAPTURES TWENTY MEN — PLANS DEFEATED, ... 238

CHAPTER XXVII.
MOSBY PROMOTED TO THE OFFICE OF LIEUTENANT-COLONEL — CHAPMAN AND MONTJOY PUNISH A GANG OF INCENDIARIES — UNSUCCESSFUL ATTACKS, . . 246

CHAPTER XXVIII.
BEHAVIOR OF THE ENEMY AT MIDDLEBURG — A BLAZE AMONG MOSBY'S MEN — CAPTAIN SAM CHAPMAN ROUTS THE SIXTH NEW YORK CAVALRY — MOSBY WOUNDED — LIEUTENANT GLASSCOCK IN SHERIDAN'S CAMP, . . . 253

CHAPTER XXIX.
SUCCESSFUL TRIPS OF LIEUTENANT RUSSELL AND COMPANIONS — THE WRITER'S VISIT TO RICHMOND — DECLINES URGENT INVITATIONS TO MAKE HIS HOME IN THE INTRENCHMENTS — MOSBY ATTACKS THE ENEMY AT SALEM — VARIOUS CAPTURES, ETC., ... 260

CHAPTER XXX.
UNITED STATES MAIL-TRAIN CAPTURED — "GOING THROUGH" THE PASSENGERS — CAPTURE OF MOSBY'S ARTILLERY — TRAINS THROWN OFF THE TRACK — GENERAL AUGER ARRESTS FIVE CITIZENS — CRUELTY, ... 270

CHAPTER XXXI.

TOO MUCH OF A GOOD THING — TREACHERY — TOO MUCH OF A GOOD THING AGAIN — CAPTAIN FRANKLAND FAILS TO "MAKE HIS JACK," 276

CHAPTER XXXII.

CAPTAIN BRASHER'S EXPEDITION INTO THE CONFEDERACY — GENERAL POWELL'S RAID — RETALIATION — EFFECTS OF RETALIATION — CASE OF ROBERT HARDOVER, 285

CHAPTER XXXIII.

ESCAPES FROM PRISON — HALL'S ESCAPE — MAGNER'S ESCAPE — ELIMINATION OF SKULKERS — MONTJOY LEARNS SOMETHING ABOUT BRASHER, ... 293

CHAPTER XXXIV.

THE BRAVE BRASHER DEFEATED AND TAKEN PRISONER — MAGNANIMITY OF BRAVE MEN — CAPTURES — CAPTURES RE-CAPTURED — ESCAPE OF YOUNG BOLLING, 299

CHAPTER XXXV.

DEATH OF MONTJOY — BURNING OF JOE BLACKWELL'S HOUSE, MOSBY'S HEADQUARTERS — A LOYAL TRANSACTION IN WOOL — RAID OF CUSTAR AND OTHERS — DESTRUCTION AND DESOLATION, ... 305

CHAPTER XXXVI.

INTENSE COLD INTERFERES WITH OPERATIONS — MOSBY SEVERELY WOUNDED — DILIGENT SEARCH FOR HIM — THE NEST WARM, BUT THE BIRD FLOWN — PROMOTIONS — "FEAST OF REASON," ETC. — MAJOR RICHARDS "PROCURES SUPPLIES," 313

CHAPTER XXXVII.

EXPLOITS OF MAJOR RICHARDS — RUMORS OF PEACE NEGOTIATIONS — DEEP SNOW — FOX-HUNTING — MAJOR GIBSON AND LIEUTENANT BAKER AFTER US — SOME OF THEM RETURN — NOBLE CONDUCT OF LIEUTENANT BAKER, ... 330

CHAPTER XXXVIII.

HIGH PRICES — FORAGING — SHERIDAN'S MARCH — MOSBY PREVENTED FROM FOLLOWING BY SWOLLEN STREAMS — EXPLOITS OF CAPTAIN GLASSCOCK AND LIEUTENANT THOMPSON — A CHALLENGE NOT ACCEPTED — DESTRUCTION OF DISTILLERIES, ... 342

CHAPTER XXXIX.

NEWS OF THE FALL OF RICHMOND — ORGANIZATION OF A NEW COMPANY — EXPLOIT OF CAPTAIN BAYLOR, ... 352

CHAPTER XL.

GLOOM PRODUCED BY THE FALL OF RICHMOND — MOSBY CONTINUES IN THE FIELD — BAYLOR'S UNWILLING RETREAT — ATTEMPT TO CAPTURE SCHOONERS — MOSBY INVITED TO SURRENDER — SOLDIERLY CONDUCT OF FEDERAL OFFICERS, . 356

CHAPTER XLI.

MOSBY DISBANDS HIS FORCES AT SALEM — FAREWELL — MOSBY TAKES THE OATH — TEN THOUSAND DOLLAR PATRIOTISM — SUBMISSION OF MOSBY'S MEN — CONCLUDING REFLECTIONS, ... 365

MOSBY AND HIS MEN.

CHAPTER I.

THE SITUATION — BOMBARDMENT OF FORT SUMTER — PRESIDENT LINCOLN'S PROCLAMATION — RIOT IN BALTIMORE — PERFIDY OF THE GOVERNOR OF MARYLAND — TREATMENT OF THE CITIZENS OF BALTIMORE.

THE American people have just passed through a great civil war, — a war that has exceeded in gigantic proportions all the great conflicts of modern times. In its swift course of destruction it has laid many fair cities in ashes, and has left to mark its course scenes of ruin and desolation that no pencil can sketch, no pen portray.

A quarter of a million of bodies that lie mouldering in Southern soil, and the thousand of widows and orphans mourning over the loss of loved ones who will never return, attest its ferocity and the earnestness with which both sections of the country fought this contest. But it is over at last. The thunder of artillery is no longer heard, and the torch of the incendiary is no longer wantonly applied to private residences, compelling the inmates to fly from the homes of their nativity to escape the insults of a licentious soldiery. The last stray shot of a guerilla has been fired, and not a single armed foe raises his hand against Federal authority. Peace has spread her smiling wings over this once fair and glorious country, and men of all parties and all classes hail with delight the prospect of once more returning to the quiet avocations of every-day life. It will take many long years of persevering industry and unremitting toil to build up the waste places that have been made almost a wilderness. It will be many years before the wounds made by this unhappy strife will be healed over; but wise councils and a spirit of moderation on the part of the Government may yet repair the mistakes of the past, and the influence of commerce, that great peacemaker, may unite the interests of both sections in an indissoluble bond, and the Sunny South may again blossom as the rose, and her power and influence be felt in the nation as of old.

The dream of Southern independence and a separate nationality has vanished forever. The cause which the men of the South had nearest their hearts, and for which they sacrificed so many lives, so much wealth, and their whole energies both of mind and body, *has failed*, their sacrifices have all been in vain, their resources have been exhausted in the fruitless endeavor to achieve their independence, and thousands of their bravest and noblest sons have fallen in the unequal contest. At the end of four years of almost superhuman exertions, they find themselves a conquered people, with the loss of every thing but their honor, seeking restoration to their former position under the Federal flag.

I was for four years in the Confederacy, having gone South almost at the very inception of the war, and having spent the last two years in guerilla warfare, in the border counties of Virginia, half of that time almost within sight of the Capital of the United States. I propose, as a part of the history of the rebellion, to give my readers a sketch of some of its main incidents, and more particularly of some of the exploits of the battalion to which I belonged, which was, from its formation to the close of the war, a terror to all the outposts and detached divisions of the Federal army, and whose scouts and couriers gave to General Lee the most, if not all, of the reliable information he received of the enemy's movements and designs, and which enabled his lieutenant-generals to deal such sudden and heavy blows upon his adversaries. The life of a guerilla is a dangerous one, but it has its charms. Its independence and freedom from restraint, and, above all, the opportunity for bold and daring actions, which carry with them personal renown, makes this life far preferable to a position in the regular army, where men stand up like posts to be shot at, and where there is little or no opportunity for the display of personal courage.

It was in April, 1861, that the first scenes of the bloody drama were enacted. I had been holding an office in the Treasury Department at Washington for the seven years previous, and was in the civil service of the Government at the time Fort Sumter was bombarded and surrendered to the Confederates under General Beauregard. The event created the most intense excitement all over the country, and no one knew what turn affairs would take. Three Confederate commissioners had been sent to Washington to negotiate for the surrender of the Southern forts, arsenals, and public property of every description, and to arrange the basis for a convention between the two Governments. They had been received informally, but their mission failed with President Buchanan. They had gone home unmolested, and the policy of the new administration had not been developed. Two of the leading Northern journals, of opposite politics, the *New York Tribune* and the *New York Herald*, were in favor of letting the South go peaceably. The Democratic party was opposed to coercion, believing that the conquest of the South was impossible, and that the country would be ruined by the war and our institutions overthrown. The Republicans, an entirely sectional party, elected on a sectional platform and for the first time in power, flushed with victory over their opponents, thought otherwise; but still they paused and hesitated before they plunged the country into a war the end of which no man could tell. Things were in this condition when the news came North that Fort Sumter had been bombarded and had fallen. It threw the whole country, North and South, into a fever of excitement, and determined the course of the new administration at once. President Lincoln issued his proclamation on the 15th day of April, 1861, calling for *seventy-five thousand men for the term of three months*, to put down the insurrection. Massachusetts was the first State to respond to the call, and in the month of April she sent two regiments to guard Washington city; for at that time it was supposed the Confederates meditated an attack upon the Capital, and so little was known concerning the plans of the Southerners and the exact condition of affairs in that section, that the report was started and actually believed by General Scott, the Government officials, and the whole North, that Ben McCulloch was marching through Virginia with five thousand Texan Rangers, supported by a large army of volunteers, on Washington, with the intention of sacking the city, destroying the public buildings, and moving northward with fire and sword. All the roads and by-paths to the city were strongly picketed. Two companies of infantry, with artillery, were posted at the long bridge across the Potomac, to prevent any attack from that point; when the actual fact was, that with the exception of two companies in Alexandria and a picket of Confederates on the Virginia side of the bridge, including a few stragglers who had come in, there was not an armed force in the field in the whole State of Virginia,—so little did the public or the Government know what was really going on in the South.

A Massachusetts regiment, passing through Baltimore on the 17th of April 1861, was attacked by a mob. Several were killed and wounded. Baltimore had always been noted for its mobocratic tendencies, and little attention was paid to the affair by the citizens, the majority of whom knew nothing of the difficulty. The regiment got through the city, however, but as the train was passing through the suburbs of the city, a member of the regiment levelled his gun, fired, and killed a highly respectable citizen (Mr. Kyle, who happened to be conversing with two or three friends) in cold blood. The news soon spread, and in a few hours the whole city of Baltimore was in a state of excitement bordering upon frenzy. The populace rose up as one man, and demanded justice in behalf of the murdered citizen. The perpetrator of the deed was not delivered up. The excitement increased. A mob collected, and the first act was to cut off all communication north of Baltimore. In one night all the railroad bridges between Baltimore and Wilmington and Harrisburg were burned and destroyed. The road between Washington Junction and Annapolis had been torn up, and the Capital of the nation was thus entirely severed from all communication with the outer world.

Had the Confederate leaders dreamed that the Federal Government intended actually to open hostilities, the State of Virginia could have thrown fifty thousand men into Maryland, taken possession of the whole State, including the District of Columbia and the Capital, and thus have ended the war, and saved all the blood and treasure that has since been wasted and squandered with such unprecedented prodigality. But they let slip the chance; they were unprepared, and a great opportunity was lost. Neither side seemed to appreciate the magnitude of the events which must necessarily have followed from what was occurring. The administration and the North thought seventy-five thousand men would quell the insurrection in three months; and the South had conceived the idea that they would, in that time, win their independence with little difficulty, and thus we gradually drifted into this great war. Neither side had counted the real cost. The South was fearfully in earnest, but they overrated their real strength and under-estimated the power of their adversaries.

But to return to Baltimore. The people held a meeting at Monument Square, and resolved that no more troops should pass through the State. The city was under military rule, and twenty thousand citizens with muskets in their hands stood ready to see that their resolutions were respected. The Governor of the State addressed them from the rostrum, and assured them that he would sooner see his own right arm torn from its socket than to allow any more men to go through the State, or to aid the Government in opposing the South. How well he kept his word was seen when, a night or two afterwards, he slipped off to Washington and was in secret consultation with Lincoln and the Secretary of War as to the best means of delivering up his own native city to the Federal authorities. He admirably succeeded and was no doubt rewarded. A short time afterwards this same Governor of a sovereign State, whose Constitution and laws he had solemnly sworn to support, we find the prime mover and instigator in the infamous plot to destroy the State Government. The Legislature was *prorogued*, and the leading members arrested and imprisoned in Fort Lafayette in New York Harbor, there to languish within the confines of damp prison walls for months without trial. They were committed, and to this day no specific charges have ever been made against them. They were finally released and allowed to return to their homes, shattered in health, and almost exiles in their own land, under the surveillance of Government detectives, and subject to all the petty malice of provost-marshals, whose chief aim seemed to be to study how to exasperate the citizens of that devoted State, which for four years had been subject to all the ignominy and wrong that governmental parasites and a few native-born renegades could heap upon her. No wonder that the sons of Maryland flocked by thousands to the Southern standard to escape from such a galling despotism at home, and rushed, with avidity, to fight for that cause that commanded their sympathy and respect.

All over the North the boast was made that Baltimore should be laid in ashes. The guns of Fort McHenry were turned upon the city, her citizens were hunted down like outlaws, men were knocked down in the streets by armed ruffians wearing the Federal uniform, houses were broken open, ladies' wardrobes were ransacked, and the owners insulted, private property was confiscated to the personal use of the soldiery, and to all these wrongs and outrages the Government manifested a stolid indifference that would have done honor to the Czar of Russia. Simply to be known to possess Southern opinions was cause enough to be thrown into a dungeon; and many a man, for the indiscreet expression of an opinion as to the legality of the high-minded measures then being enacted, was dragged from his bed and the bosom of his family, at the dead hour of midnight, and hurried off to provost-marshals, and, without a hearing, immediately transferred to some Government prison. It created no surprise that Maryland was disaffected and still is so, for she has had nothing for which to thank the United States Government.

CHAPTER II.

EXCITEMENT IN WASHINGTON — GOVERNMENT CLERKS CALLED UPON TO ENROLL THEMSELVES — AUTHOR LEAVES WASHINGTON — ARRIVES IN MONTGOMERY — ENTHUSIASM OF THE SOUTHERN PEOPLE — SEAT OF GOVERNMENT REMOVED TO RICHMOND.

WASHINGTON CITY was in a state of ferment and confusion. There were not more than two thousand troops there to guard the Capital of the Nation. The President and Cabinet were frightened at their supposed danger. The Government clerks were called upon to enroll themselves into companies for the common protection. Arms were distributed all through the departments and stacked in every room, to be used at a moment's warning. The notorious Jim Lane of Kansas, with one hundred of his desperadoes, bivouacked in the East Room of the White House, as a body guard for his Excellency the President, and all day long the click of the hammer and chisel could be heard in the basements of the Treasury Building and Patent Office, preparing mines to blow up the public buildings and records in case of necessity. A gunboat at the Navy Yard had steam up all the time ready to bear away to a place of safety the precious lives of the head of the Government and his official advisers. During this time Southerners in Washington were openly leaving to join the Confederate army. Southern communication had not yet been stopped, though a squad of soldiers from Alexandria were guarding the long bridge that crosses the Potomac at Washington. No attempt was made to stop these men. The Heads of the Departments caused a new test oath, unknown to the Constitution and the laws, to be administered to the clerks. Those who did not take it were summarily turned out of office. Those Southern men who took it and stayed did not remain long in office; their truculency could not save them, and the hordes of office-seekers from the New England States, who so pertinaciously beset the President and Heads of Departments, soon drove the remaining Southern democrats out in the cold, because they could not stretch themselves to the extreme measures of the radicals.

Not caring to be turned out of office I promptly sent in my resignation. I did not await its acceptance. Having packed up the night before, and bidding a few friends good-by, on Wednesday, the 25th of April, 1861, I jumped into a stage coach and started to Dixie.

As we rolled over the Long Bridge I looked back upon the city I was leaving, where I had spent so many happy hours in social intercourse with friends from all sections of the country, and I cursed, in my inmost soul, the madness and folly of a sectional fanaticism that was hastening our country, with such rapid strides, into the vortex of civil war.

The spires and cupolas of Washington, with the half-finished dome of the Capitol, soon faded in the distance, and in a half-hour's time I was in the confines of the Confederacy.

The first place we arrived at was Alexandria. Here the Stars and Bars floated proudly from almost every housetop; and it was a great relief to pass from the gloom and despondency that prevailed in Washington, to the life and animation of Alexandria. All was bustle and excitement; energy and determination were stamped upon the countenance of every man I met. They all seemed to be putting their shoulder to the wheel; and the State of Virginia, having, by a solemn ordinance, dissolved her connection with the Federal Government, and joined her fortunes to the infant republic, her sons advanced with alacrity to their support, and rushed, with enthusiasm, to enroll themselves for the defence of their native State, which was so soon to become the scene of the greatest battle of modern times. There was no flinching or holding back. The gray-haired man of sixty years, as well as the boy of sixteen summers, hastened to don the Confederate gray, and receive the congratulations of friends and brothers in arms, for the holy cause of independence which they then swore to uphold. And never did men take an oath more eagerly and with greater honesty of purpose.

For years the mad policy of the Northern politicians had been seeking to rend asunder, by their sectional onslaughts, the bonds of brotherly love that bound the North and South together. Gradually distrust and doubt, aggravated by insults and continual encroachments of the growing dominant party, settled into a firm conviction in the minds of the Southern people, that they should soon be tied hand and foot, and at the mercy of a Jacobinical party, whose genius for evil has been manifested in this country ever since the landing of the Mayflower at Plymouth Rock. The South felt this spirit of intolerance growing in the country day by day, and they resolved to break loose from this bondage, cost what it might, and be a free and independent nation. The heartfelt prayers of their entire home circles went with them, and they stood ready to march forth to do battle for their firesides and their freedom.

I left Alexandria the next morning, and proceeded to Charlottesville, *via* the Orange and Alexandria Railroad, where we arrived about noon, and found a large crowd waiting at the depot to hear the news from Washington, and to learn whether the Yankees would commence hostilities. I stayed that night with my brother at the University of Virginia located at that place, where he was completing his studies. I found, out of six hundred and fifty students, all but seventy-five had left for their homes preparatory to entering the Confederate service. The young men had cheerfully given up the ease and quiet and comforts of a student's life, and were prepared to bear and endure all the hardships, perils, and discomforts of camp-life. The deprivation of home comforts and luxuries, the dangers of the battle-field, and that worse than death, sickness in a camp hospital, were no drawback to their ardor, and all this *for independence* and a complete separation from our late Northern allies. I looked around upon the desolate halls of the University, the silent quarters of the students which a few weeks ago presented so much life and animation, and where were the occupants? Gone forth in defence of the infant Republic. And where are now those noble youths, who sprang forward with such alacrity and buoyant spirits, to the mortal encounter? A large number of them have fallen on the battle-fields of Virginia, fighting nobly for the cause they espoused; many have fallen victims to the cold and piercing lake winds on Johnson's Island, while languishing in imprisonment; and but a few of that gallant band, whose first exploit was the capture of Harper's Ferry, remain to tell the tale of what might have been.

From Charlottesville I went to Lynchburg, and found there that two of my brothers had already entered the service as privates, and were ready at a moment's warning to march to the seat of war. All the able-bodied young men of Lynchburg were volunteering, and crowds were coming in from all sides to volunteer their services for their country. The city was filled with recruits from the adjoining counties, and troops were arriving on almost every train of cars from the Gulf States, all eager for the fray, and all determined to fight it out to the bitter end. Such a scene would inspire the most lukewarm with the confidence of ultimate success. It might take years of labor and fighting, and oceans of blood and treasure; but what were these in comparison with independence and a Government of our own? These were the thoughts and feelings that animated us all; and in that crowd of people at Lynchburg, I do not believe there was a man who would not have staked his last dollar and his last acre of land upon the success of the Southern arms. I stayed in Lynchburg but one day, and the next morning at daylight set out on the Virginia and Tennessee Railroad, for Montgomery, Alabama, which was then capital of the Confederacy. All along the road, at Liberty, Wythville, Bristol, Knoxville, Dalton, and Atlanta, the people were very enthusiastic, and were determined to see that the Southern cause came out of the issue triumphant. There was no croaking and no drawing back; but every man was imbued with an inborn resolution to abide by the fortunes of the Confederacy.

I arrived at Montgomery in the early part of May, 1861. Nothing could exceed the enthusiasm of the people here. The streets were crowded with soldiers, some organized and marching through to Pensacola, others receiving their uniforms at the expense of the citizens, and waiting marching orders. The new Government was under full headway, the departments all regularly organized and in full operation, and the machinery of Government working as smoothly as in the departments at Washington. I found many familiar faces that I had seen and been in contact with in the public offices in Washington, who had followed the new Government to Montgomery. I presented my credentials in person, and was told my case would be attended to in a few days. Having resigned my office in Washington, and being perfectly familiar with all the details of the Treasury Department business, I had no doubt that I should in a few days get the same position I held under the old *regime*. Being acquainted with a number of the Representatives, and having letters of introduction to some of the leading members of Congress, I went to see them, and found a perfect unanimity of opinion as to the course the Southern States had taken, and the policy to be pursued. The die had been cast, the Rubicon passed, and with their eyes turned to the future and the Herculean efforts to be made, these men gave themselves body and soul to the accomplishment of their avowed purposes, and to make an era in the history of this continent which would redound to their glory. The first Congress of the Confederate States were fearfully in earnest, and to see their resolution and determination, no one would for a moment have supposed that the people whom they represented could ever be conquered or again bow the knee to a political master.

The next day the Virginia delegates to the Confederate Congress arrived. They were welcomed with open arms for upon the fidelity and endurance of that great State, the mother of States and statesmen, the success of the Southern cause depended. From her geographical position, upon the soil of Virginia would be fought the great battles of the war. That State would be the first one invaded, and to prevent the Federals from acquiring a foothold within her borders would require all the valor and undivided strength of her sons, as well as the whole power of the Confederate Government. Though the last State to secede from the mother Government, and so loth to part with all the blessings, recollections, and ties that sprang from a Government of which she had been the founder and so warm an adherent, yet when she did wheel into line with her sister States in a cause that bound all her sympathies and commanded all her support, she buckled on her armor, and, like the knights of old, she went into the contest with a singleness of purpose and a high sense of honor that has extorted the admiration of the world, and commanded the respect of her adversaries, even though she has fallen from her great estate in the councils of the nation since the close of the war. But her position in the history of this country can never be mistaken by intelligent minds, and the grand old Commonwealth, though she may have for a time lost her prestige, yet another generation will soon spring up, and the State that has been styled the mother of Presidents, will regain the position she has heretofore so proudly and nobly held.

With the delegates from Virginia came General Joe Johnston. He held a long consultation with President Davis and his cabinet, and urged, as a military as well as a political measure, the immediate removal of the Capital from Montgomery to Richmond.

General Johnston's council prevailed. The last week in May 1861, the Capital was moved to Richmond. I returned to Virginia, and remained in Lynchburg until the first week in June. In the meanwhile suitable buildings had been secured for the Departments of the Government, and early in June the whole machinery was working like a clock. The President took up his residence at the Spottswood Hotel, where rooms had been fitted up for him in the most elegant and complete manner. In a short time the citizens of Richmond purchased the large and splendid residence of Mr. Creushaw, at the corner of 11th Street and Lee, refurnished it from garret to cellar in the most elegant manner, and presented it, with a splendid carriage and horses, to his Excellency, which carriage, when the Confederate forces evacuated Richmond, General Ord appropriated to his own private use.

CHAPTER III.

PREPARATIONS FOR WAR IN RICHMOND—BEAUREGARD ARRIVES IN RICHMOND—BUTLER MARCHES TO BETHEL AND BACK—BATTLE OF MANASSAS—DISORDERLY RETREAT OF THE YANKEES—REJOICINGS IN RICHMOND.

DURING the organization of the Government in Richmond, preparations for a vigorous prosecution of the war were made. The greatest activity prevailed everywhere. At the old Virginia Armory the machinists were working night and day. Old flint-locks were converted into percussion-locks. The Tredegar Works were working like bees, rifling old cannon and making new ones. Troops were coming in almost every hour of the day, from all the Southern States, and amongst the first was a company, "The Davis Rangers," all the way from Louisville, Kentucky, and composed partly of young men I knew in my schoolboy days. Fitzhugh was captain, with A. Gale, Ed Cocke, Ivinny Colmesmil and Mat Gist as his lieutenants and sergeants. They encamped at the old Fair Grounds until other troops from Kentucky arrived, and when they were organized into a regiment with Tom Taylor as colonel, volunteers from the Border and Gulf States were arriving by every train of cars. Schools of instruction were established all around the city. The drill-masters could be heard every hour of the day and night instructing their men. The principal school for the instruction of the cavalry was established at Ashland, the principal instructor being Captain L. L. Lomax, afterwards Major-General of cavalry, a graduate of West Point, who had served with distinction in the regular army of the United States before the war, fighting the Indians on the frontiers, but who, on the breaking out of the war and secession of his native State, Virginia, resigned and came South. Our cavalry furnished their own horses and equipments.

The latter part of June, Beauregard arrived in Richmond and was ordered to take command of the troops at Manassas, the point to which the eyes of both North and South were directed, and on the plains of which, afterwards, two of the hardest battles of the war were fought, and two of the grandest victories won. On his arrival there the keen eyes of that great soldier, after a survey of the country, soon recognized the importance of fortifying the place, as it was one of the keys to Richmond. The Yankees had already occupied Alexandria and were fortifying Arlington Heights, the home of our great chieftain, General Robert E. Lee. The first levy of troops, seventy-five thousand men, were already in and preparing for an advance right on to Richmond. The Yankees, by some means, had conceived the idea that no resistance would be offered them on their march to Richmond; that all they had to do was to march right down and take it; and that the *Rebels* would fly from before them and scatter like chaff before the wind. Their implements of war had all the most modern improvements, while the Confederates were armed with old flint-lock muskets, except a few got at Harper's Ferry armory, and some old smoothbore pieces of artillery.

Brigadier-General Magruder was on the Peninsula at Williamsburg, with a force of not more than two thousand five hundred men watching the movements of the enemy. General Butler, better know as Beast Butler, was in command at Fortress Monroe, and to have the credit and glory of being the first one to enter the Rebel Capital, he marched out of his intrenchments on the —— day of June, 1861, to ride rough-shod and disperse the *mob* of Magruder, which seemed to offer the only obstacle in the path to Richmond, and met at Bethel with a reconnoitering force sent out by Magruder. The Confederates had only two pieces of artillery and three howitzers, commanded by Captain Randolph, afterward General, and the distinguished Secretary of War. The enemy numbered five to one. Butler ordered the attack. The Confederates stood their ground nobly, and being accustomed to the use of fire-arms, made every shot tell. The Yankees charged and charged, but could not stand the deadly fire poured into their ranks by our men. Randolph captured one of his "masked batteries," and at the first shot with grape and canister, the enemy broke and fled like sheep, leaving their dead and wounded on the field. The effect of Randolph's howitzers on the Yankees was like that which they have on the Indians, who will stand off and fight all day long with long-range guns, but the moment you thunder your artillery at them they drop their arms and fly for their lives. So it was at Bethel. The first discharge played such havoc with their ranks that they threw down their arms and ran away, thus adopting the principle of Hudibras, —

> "He who fights, and runs away,
> Will live to fight another day."

These guns of Randolph's were nothing more nor less than one of those "*masked batteries*" which were such a *bugbear* and horror to the Yankees the first year of the war. This affair, being the first battle on the seaboard, was considered a most important one in its results. The Confederates had been longing to be led against the enemy to test their mettle. It inspired the men with confidence; it instilled new vigor into their camps.

The enemy, failing in this movement, directed their attention towards Manassas. A party of their cavalry dashed into Fairfax Court House, and captured Captain Ball and nearly the whole of his men doing picket duty. It was in this affair that the gallant Marr fell while trying to rally his men in the face of an overwhelming force. Captain Ball and his men were marched into Washington City, and being the first prisoners of war ever there, they created quite a sensation. No preparation had been made in the metropolis then for the reception and detention of prisoners. They were placed under guard on board the steamboat St. Nicholas, and the officer who made the capture was promoted to a majority.

On the 19th of July the Yankees made a reconnoissance in force, on our lines, at Bull Run. Only three hundred of our men were behind the entrenchments, commanded by Colonel Smith, afterwards Governor of Virginia. The Yankees charged our men several times, but were repulsed with heavy loss, and retreated in great confusion. On the 21st of July the first and one of the hardest fought battles of the war was fought at Manassas. The enemy, having completed all their arrangements, advanced with thirty-five thousand men, under McDowell, and commenced the attack on us at daylight. The battle raged with the greatest fury, the advantage being first on one side then on the other, until five o'clock in the afternoon, when Stonewall Jackson and Kirby Smith came up on our left and determined the fortunes of the day. The result would have been determined sooner had it not been for the treachery of the conductor of the train, who had been bribed by the enemy to delay the train and prevent the junction with Beauregard. The conductor was bribed by the Yankees to delay the train, by paying him five hundred dollars in gold. On the approach of the train to Manassas, the cannonading could be distinctly heard for a distance of ten or fifteen miles. The eagerness of our men to engage the enemy was so great that the train was stopped ten miles from the scene of action, and the men double-quicked it from there to the field. On our right and centre we were hardest pushed, and were nearly broken down by fighting all day. Our ranks were terribly thinned, the enemy gradually pushing them back, yet every man was fighting like a hero. Indeed, so hard pushed were the Confederates, that General Beauregard sent back orders to Manassas to prepare the works for his men, as he intended to fall back to his fortifications.

While all this was going on, a shout was heard in the distance on our left. The idea of being flanked had seized the minds of the men, and everything looked indeed gloomy. The shout approached nearer, and just at the moment when Beauregard and Johnson were conferring what to do, a courier dashed up, bringing intelligence of the arrival of Kirby Smith and Jackson with two thousand five hundred reënforcements. The intelligence soon spread through the army. A new life was infused into that body of heroes; a final charge was ordered, and those weary, broken-down, and disheartened men responded to it with the alacrity of fresh soldiers. On the left Smith and Jackson's men stopped to form, and charged (half of them without bayonets on their guns) with a yell which seemed to shake the very earth. The enemy broke and ran, followed by our men. Pressed so hard, divesting themselves of every incumbrance, they fled in the greatest disorder, and did not stop until they reached Alexandria and Washington. After a few minutes' pursuit by our cavalry, their wagon-train was overtaken; horses and mules were taken from it by the horror-stricken Yankees, to facilitate and make good their retreat, or, in fact, *flight*. The roads became blocked up with deserted and broken-down wagons, artillery, and caissons. At Fairfax Court House a Congressional party and some *ladies* had come out to witness the carnage and celebrate their victory with a splendid banquet at Manassas, and follow on with the army in their triumphal march and entry into Richmond. They, however, never realized their bright dreams. Several members of the party, including a Congressman (Mr. Ely), were captured with all their *nice things*, wines, liquors, &c., and sent to Richmond by railroad.

President Davis left Richmond Sunday morning for Manassas, and arrived there at the most critical period of the battle. A number of our best officers had fallen; our ranks so thinned that the only hope there seemed to be left for us was behind the fortifications. He rode on the field, and encouraged the men by his words and actions. That Sunday was an eventful day in the history of Richmond, and will be long remembered. None but the authorities knew that the hardest-fought battle of the war was going on then. A strange spell seemed to hang over the people. Every one was inquiring, "What's the matter?" Something important was going on. "The President was not at church." About noon telegrams were received for all the troops in Richmond to get ready to move at a moment's notice. About five o'clock P.M., Mrs. Davis received a dispatch from the President that "a great battle was going on." The news spread like wildfire. The people flocked to Main Street and the hotels to get some intelligence. About eight o'clock P.M., telegrams were received from the President announcing "a great but dear-bought victory." "The enemy are flying in every direction, and our cavalry in hot pursuit." On this being known, the enthusiasm of the people knew no bounds. Bells were rung, salutes fired, &c., &c.

The next day the wounded began to arrive. The hospital accommodations being very limited, the citizens took the wounded heroes to their own houses and nursed them. I went up to visit the battle-field three days after, to look after my brothers. The slaughter of the enemy was very great, for on

Wednesday, three days after the battle, large numbers of the enemy were unburied, most of them Ellsworth Zouaves. Major Haywood, of General Beauregard's staff, kindly furnished me with a horse, which enabled me to view the whole battle-field. The point where Sherman's celebrated battery was captured bore the strongest evidence of the desperation with which the combatants fought. There were seen the wheels of broken caissons, &c., perforated with musket balls, horses shot through and through, — scrub-oaks and pine-bushes with tops shot off, — men headless, &c.

CHAPTER IV.

MCCLELLAN'S ANACONDA — ACCOUNT OF MOSBY'S FAMILY AND EARLY LIFE — MOSBY RESPONDS TO THE CALL OF THE GOVERNOR — BATTLE OF SEVEN PINES — MOSBY PENETRATES THE LINES OF THE ENEMY, AND LEARNS MCCLELLAN'S PLANS — BOLD ESCAPE.

EVERYTHING remained tranquil in Richmond until the next spring, when McClellan commenced the execution of his *Anaconda* system, when by one simultaneous strike by the armies of the Potomac, the Cumberland, and that west of the Mississippi, the Confederate armies were to be crushed and dispersed. It was about this time, March, 1862, that the hero of this book attracted the attention of his superior officers.

This truly celebrated man, John Singleton Mosby, was born at "Edgemont," Powhatan County, Virginia, on the 6th day of December, 1833. The place of his birth was one of those beautiful country-seats, peculiar to that region, and was owned by Colonel Mosby's grandfather, James McLaurine. His father was Alfred D. Mosby, a native of Nelson County, Virginia, and a graduate of Hampden Sidney College. Colonel Mosby's mother was a Miss Virginia I. McLaurine, who belonged to one of the best families in the State.

Mr. Alfred D. Mosby, his father, resided in Nelson County, until John was about five years of age, when he purchased "Tudor Grove," one of those lovely country residences which abound around Charlottesville, Virginia. There he resided until John was nineteen years old, when he sold out, and moved to Amherst County. John was the oldest child of his parents, and when a boy, exhibited those traits of character and energy which marked so strongly his later years. Having received a most excellent primary education, at the early age of sixteen years he entered the University of Virginia. Here he made extraordinary progress, graduating in the Greek course the first year, and being the only one who did so that session. He remained there during the years 1851, 1852, and part of 1853, when he graduated with the highest honors. While there he enjoyed the confidence and esteem of the professors;

and Dr. Gesner Harrison frequently remarked that John Mosby would make his mark in life, and that he was one of the most clever young men he had ever known among the students at the University. He was warm-hearted and high-spirited, and consequently had many warm friends and bitter enemies; but he was never known to forsake a friend in time of need. He is generous to a fault, as his coming out of the war poorer than when he went in abundantly proves. And out of all the prisoners he captured, not one can say that Mosby robbed him. After leaving the University he studied law, and commenced the practice of his profession in Howardsville, Albermarle County, with great success. When quite young he married in Nashville, Tennessee, on the 30th of December, 1857, Miss Pauline Clark, daughter of the Hon. Beverly L. Clark, of Kentucky, and late Minister to Central America. He settled then in Goodson, Washington County, Virginia, and resumed the practice of his profession with extraordinary success, soon ranking as one of the leading members of the bar, and among that number Colonel Goodson stood foremost.

A. E. RICHARDS.

In 1860, signs of national troubles began to be visible in the horizon. The seeds of discord which the fanatics of New England had been sowing for forty years had so thoroughly poisoned the minds of the people in the Northern States that a civil war seemed inevitable. The people of Virginia had exhausted every means of saving the country from the whirlpool into which the New England politicians and fanatics were driving it, and there was no alternative left for the sons of the South but to buckle on their armor and fight it out. Mosby was among the first who responded to the call of the Governor for troops to resist the invaders of her soil, by shouldering his gun and volunteering as a private in the First Regiment of Virginia Cavalry. His popularity was so great, and his friends reposed such confidence in him, that the citizens of the county presented him with a fine charger, to commence with, and well has he proved himself worthy of that confidence.

But I must return to my narrative. Our Cavalry were picketing in Fairfax and Prince William Counties in March 1862. The Yankees commenced their advance. Mosby, while out scouting near the Potomac River, saw a large column of the enemy moving in a strange direction; he returned immediately, reported the fact to General Stuart, and volunteered to ascertain the object of it. Stuart gave him two men, and out they started. He penetrated the enemy's lines. He went to General Heintzelman's headquarters, and just missed him. While there he found out, from officers on Heintzelman's Staff, the whole of McClellan's plans. Distrusting them, he was provided with passes, and went down to see for himself. He found their statement correct. He returned to Stuart, and reported McClellan transporting his troops to the Peninsula — and the column he saw moving was to deceive our army. In consequence of this intelligence, Johnson and Beauregard determined on an immediate evacuation of Manassas and Centreville. In a few hours the Confederate army was moving to the Peninsula *via* Richmond. The evacuation was not an hour too soon. By the time Longstreet had arrived at Williamsburg to reënforce Magruder, McClellan with one hundred and thirty-five thousand men, had landed at Fortress Monroe and was moving up the

Peninsula. An engagement ensued at Williamsburg, a portion of McClellan's army was driven back by one division under Longstreet, who was compelled to fall back on account of the danger of being flanked by the enemy's gunboats. At West Point General Franklin's corps was repulsed by a Texas brigade. Yet McClellan telegraphed to Washington, that he was " pushing Johnston to the wall," and *" that a few hours' march would bring him to Richmond."* A great deal of apprehension that the city would be evacuated, prevailed in Richmond. General Johnson determined by one bold stroke to annihilate his adversary.

The battle of Seven Pines was fought, and but for the wounding of General Johnston on the second day's fight, there can be no question in the minds of any military man, that McClellan's army would have been destroyed. The watercourses ran high, and the country was flooded with water. Our men fought in the swamps with water and mud up to their knees. General Johnston was wounded Sunday morning, the second day's fighting. On Saturday the battle commenced before noon. The thunder of artillery and rattling of musketry could be distinctly heard in the city.

Hundreds of citizens flocked to the roof of the Capitol from which, with the aid of glasses, could be seen in the swamps of the Chickahominy, the bursting of the shells, &c. The battles ceased Sunday about ten o'clock A.M. General Johnston was carried into Richmond to receive medical aid, his wound not being very dangerous; but he got three of his ribs broken by falling from his horse. General Lee assumed command of the army. He reorganized it — and enforced discipline, recruited his army, and fortified himself. Fears were entertained in Richmond by the citizens that McClellan would get in. Large numbers left the place; some ran off and left their houses vacant, while others sold out at a great sacrifice.

About this time the name of *Jeb* Stuart had got to be a terror to the enemy, and while McClellan was lying around Richmond, Mosby proposed to General Stuart to make a raid around McClellan's army. Stuart requested him to put his plans in writing, which he did, and Stuart submitted them to General Lee. He approved it and authorized Mosby to take as many men as he wanted. He took two with him, and passing through Dr. Price's farm was chased by the Second United States Dragoons until dark, and the party escaped. The scouting was resumed the next day. When near the Richmond and York River Railroad, they met the same regiment drawn up in line of battle. There was no chance of escape, and knowing their dread of Stuart he rode out with his men in full view of the enemy, and raising himself in his saddle, and looking back and beckoning with his hat, cried out at the top of his voice, which made the very welkin ring, "*Here they are Jeb!*" The enemy, concluding Stuart was in the woods near by with his whole cavalry force, broke and ran away, with Mosby and his two men after them. The Major of the regiment was killed, and his fine gray horse captured and brought to Stuart's headquarters. Mosby was complimented for this daring act, and presented with the horse.

CHAPTER V.

MOSBY'S RAID ROUND THE ENEMY—IS TAKEN PRISONER—BATTLE OF HARRISON'S LANDING — STONEWALL JACKSON'S VISIT TO RICHMOND — MOSBY EXCHANGED — POPE DEFEATED — HOOKER DEFEATED.

LEE and Stuart being convinced of the practicability of Mosby's plan for a raid round the enemy's army, one was determined on. The country is familiar with that brilliant achievement, how Stuart and his men swam the rising Chickahominy, &c., &c., and returned to our lines without losing a man. Mosby was Stuart's guide on that occasion. General Lee having completed all his arrangements for an advance, started Mosby with important verbal dispatches, to General Jackson, and while resting his horse at Beaver Dam Station, on the Virginia Central Railroad, the enemy dashed in and took him prisoner. Being suspected to be a courier with important dispatches, he was searched diligently; but none were found, and he frightened the enemy away from the railroad by telling them a train of cars, loaded with infantry and artillery, would be there in a few minutes. They retreated precipitately. Mosby was carried to General McCook's headquarters, and was asked where Jackson and Stuart were. "*He didn't know*," and "*couldn't see it*." He was then sent to Washington guarded by seven men. His fame as one of Stuart's principal scouts had already reached the Yankee army. He was kindly treated. Lee was concentrating his whole strength around Richmond, and his army did not exceed eighty thousand men. While strengthening himself thus, Jackson was sweeping everything before him in the Valley, and as a blind to the enemy, General Lee dispatched Whiting's division to Staunton to *reënforce* him; they, however, returned by rail on the next train.

General Lee's plans being now completed, by an arrangement, Jackson, after having driven the enemy out of the Valley, swept, as if by magic, down the railroad to General Lee's left, and rested his army six hours at Ashland on the Fredericksburg and Potomac Railroad. One hour after his arrival there, he rode into Richmond at midnight, with no one but an orderly, conferred with the President and General Lee, and returned to commence the attack at daylight the next morning. The signal for the attack was the firing of three guns. General Lee commenced the attack, the signal was given, the firing of three guns, and promptly did Jackson respond. Then the fighting extended along the whole line of both armies. The Yankees unexpectedly found an army in their rear, as if they had dropped down from the clouds. The utmost confusion prevailed in the ranks of the enemy. On pressed the *Stonewall*, his men mowing down the enemy. Their battle-cry "Jackson," acted as magic on the enemy. They could not realize that an army which, twenty-fours before, was five hundred miles from them, with the Big Blue Ridge Mountains between, would now be behind them, inflicting the same deadly blows on them they had dealt on their friends in the Valley. Yet it was a fearful reality to them. They retreated; they fled like chaff before the wind. McClellan, who proudly boasted he would capture* the city without firing a gun, was

---

* See his Dispatches.

now skulking, like a whipped dog, in the morass around Harrison's Landing.

Richmond was free once more from the menace of a merciless foe. The people, who a few days before, were gloomy and almost despaired of ever realizing their hope of an independent government by reason of the disasters to our arms in the West, under the great Albert Sydney Johnston, who sacrificed his life in vindicating his character as a soldier, against the malicious and dishonorable insinuations of the politicians and croakers, and the fall of McIntosh and McCullough in Arkansas, were now reanimated. Business revived, and citizens who had abandoned their property returned. Recruits began to come in rapidly.

The Sunday after the seven days' battle around Richmond, Generals Lee, Jackson, Longstreet, Polk, and others, attended divine worship in Richmond. This was Jackson's first visit to Richmond since the commencement of the war. The anxiety of the people to see this remarkable man was so great, that as soon as it was known he was at Dr. Hayes' church, a large crowd assembled in front of it to see him when he came out. Nothing would satisfy them short of shaking hands with him. And so strong was their attachment for him they cut all the buttons off his coat. The crowd was increasing every moment, but the crazy General would not gratify all of them. He broke through the crowd, and, taking the arm of a friend, went home with him. The next day he returned to his division.

Heretofore the Yankees would entertain no proposition leading to an exchange of prisoners, but now their great "*Little Mac*" had been beaten so badly and lost nearly half of his army, they were inclined to come to terms on that point. Every available warehouse and vacant building was filled with their wounded and prisoners; and they had become not only a burthen on the Government, but a nuisance to the people. Accordingly, a cartel for the exchange of prisoners was agreed upon, and amongst the first exchanged, was John S. Mosby. The vessel he was on, when it reached Fortress Monroe, was detained several days in consequence of important military movements going on. During that detention none of the prisoners were allowed to go on deck. Mosby, looking through one of the port-holes of the vessel, discovered vessels, loaded with troops, moving; and he determined, if possible, to find out what it meant. Conceiving the idea that McClellan was evacuating Harrison's Landing, he by some means got on deck, and saw the captain of the vessel. A conversation ensued between them, and Mosby's voice having a little of that twang which is peculiar to the Yankees, he easily ingratiated himself into the confidence of the captain of the boat, who told him he had been engaged a week in carrying troops from Harrison's Landing. The next day the vessel he was on started for City Point, where he was exchanged. He mounted a horse as soon as he got ashore, and rode that night to General Lee's headquarters, and informed him of the movements of the enemy. General Lee complimented him for his intelligence, &c., &c. The next morning the whole Confederate army was set in motion, and on the march. Richmond was relieved of the swarms of soldiers that infested the place while the army was around it. There is nothing more injurious to an army than to be quartered near a large city.

Soon after these important events had

occurred around Richmond, McClellan was relieved of his command, and General Pope, the General whose " headquarters were in the saddle, and whose back was never turned on the enemy," took command of the *finest army the sun ever shone upon*, — the Army of the Potomac. My readers are perfectly familiar with his *brilliant* but brief career; how he went up like a sky-rocket and came down like a stick; how the second battle of Manassas would have been won had certain generals carried out certain orders of his, &c., &c. Jackson played the same prominent part in this battle that he did in those around Richmond. While Longstreet engaged the enemy in Thoroughfare Gap, Jackson crossed the Bull Run Mountains lower down, at Aldie. Longstreet then threw a small force through Hopwell Gap, thus flanking the enemy. The Yankees retreated in confusion, and were followed up by Longstreet with his whole force. The thundering of the artillery in the distance told with what fury the battle was raging. Jackson was hard-pressed, but his men stood their ground. Soon Longstreet reënforced him, and the slaughter of the enemy then it is fearful to think of now. They were routed; Pope himself left all his personal effects, including official papers, &c., and escaped in his shirtsleeves. In his flight he left his sword behind to be captured by Lieutenant Charles Minnigerode, son of Rev. Mr. Minnigerode, pastor of St. Paul's Church in Richmond.

In Richmond the greatest enthusiasm prevailed, and hopes were entertained of a speedy termination of the war. Trade revived, and new recruits came in to give the invasion of the South the finishing blow. After a short time of rest given the army, General Lee invaded Maryland. The battles of Boonsboro', Antietam, and Sharpsburg were fought. The hard fighting of this campaign, with the long and rapid marches, had nearly exhausted the troops. At Antietam the battle was a drawn one, and no victory to the enemy. If they claim it, why did not the enemy follow up their success? They incurred such a loss as to render a pursuit impracticable. General Lee recrossed the Potomac, and took a position on the Rappahannock and went into winter quarters. Fighting Joe Hooker was put in command of the Army of the Potomac. He occupied Falmouth opposite Fredericks-

burg, and attempted to scatter Lee's army at
the Wilderness in the winter. He led his
men into a slaughter-pen. They were horribly
butchered, and left thousands of prisoners.
Great alarm prevailed in Washington. The
President and his Cabinet prepared at once
to leave the city. Urgent appeals were
made to the people to send in reënforcements
to defend the Capital. The draft was inadequate to furnish men fast enough for Southern bullets. The Governors of the different
Northern States (particularly the Governor
of Pennsylvania) called out the whole militia
force of the State. This battle of the Wilderness was the severest blow the Yankees
had yet received. The Border States were
apprehensive the rebels would wage a war of
invasion the next campaign. They were not
mistaken in their apprehensions; for during
the remainder of the winter General Lee was
concentrating all his available men for the
purpose of carrying the war into the enemy's
own country.

CHAPTER VI.

MOSBY RECEIVES HIS COMMISSION AS CAPTAIN — KILPATRICK AND DAHLGREN — ALARM IN RICHMOND — HOOKER'S DEFEAT — DEATH OF STONEWALL JACKSON — SORROW OF THE SOUTHERN PEOPLE.

IT was this winter, or rather during the month of March, that Mosby received his commission as captain in the Confederate States army, and authority to wage a partisan ranger war on the enemy. General Stuart first gave him fifteen men, and then increased the number to thirty, with privilege to select his own men. Generals Lee and Stuart both knew the value of Mosby as a scout, and the invaluable service he would render them in that capacity. They also authorized him to raise his company to the full quota. So when the spring campaign opened he had but thirty men.

While these preparations were going on, Burnside took command of the Union army, then lying on the hills of Stafford opposite Fredericksburg. While there, Kilpatrick and Dahlgren make their celebrated raid on Richmond, and in which the latter lost his life. On Dahlgren's body was found a copy of the orders he was directed to execute. The substance of them was, they were to institute an indiscriminate slaughter of the innocent people of Richmond, including the President and his Cabinet, and to set fire to the public buildings. But Providence decreed otherwise. Dahlgren lost his way and was obliged to fly through the lower counties. In King and Queen County there were a few regular soldiers at their homes on furlough, who got together and determined to harass and do them all the damage they could, and knowing the road Dahlgren would take, they determined to lie in ambush for him. Presently the Federal troops came along, Dahlgren with four or five men in advance. Hearing a rustling in the leaves, Dahlgren demands a surrender. The response he received was a volley from the Confederates. Dahlgren fell from his horse lifeless. His comrades fell back to the main column, and without a guide, in a hostile country, and their main reliance, Dahlgren, killed, the remaining officers held a consultation, and concluded to surrender, first killing their horses and destroying their weapons. Some prisoners of ours they held, however, persuaded them not to do such an insane act; that if they did, they would forfeit the respect due to prisoners of war, and would most certainly be killed. Their councils prevailed, and they surrendered the next morning to thirty men under the command of Captain ———, and were marched up to Richmond and furnished with accommodations in the Libby. The orders were published, and the citizens of Richmond were perfectly amazed at the fate they had escaped, and could scarcely believe that any one in the nineteenth century was capable of such a diabolical scheme. Dahlgren's body — *minus* his çork leg — was brought to Richmond for identification, and buried in Potter's Field.

Kilpatrick, however, was more fortunate. He penetrated our lines on the Brooke Turnpike as far as the Hon. James Lyon's residence, and a mile and a half from Richmond, and in full view of its State House, spires, and public buildings. On reaching this point, the last line of breastworks between them and the city, and behind which there were not one hundred men, he threw himself at the head of his men, pulled off his hat, and pointing with it to the city, cried out, "*Follow me, men, and in five minutes we will have the city.*" Why they did not follow their general I have never learned. They could not realize the fact that the city at that moment lay at their mercy. They seemed spellbound, and sat on their horses like mummies. They doubtless would have followed their general, but they must have imagined there were *some masked* batteries between that point and the city, but no piece of artillery was nearer them than the city, and only one company of infantry behind the breastworks at the time they were drawn up in line of battle before them. If they had got into the city, I doubt very much whether any would have got out alive. Every man in the city had a musket, and in two minutes' time artillery could have been placed in position to have raked every street. The demonstration of the enemy at this point was entirely unexpected by those in authority. They had had no intimation of this raid, for when this demonstration was made there was not a single piece of artillery behind this inner line of works. The greatest excitement prevailed in Richmond. The town bell was rung, and the citizens were soon under arms and marching out to the intrenchments by companies and battalions, to resist and drive back the incendiaries and invaders.

This winter the star of the Army of Northern Virginia was at its zenith. The army lay on the banks of the Rappahannock River, prouder and more defiant than ever. General Hooker had assumed command of the Army of the Potomac. Before the Congressional Committee on the War, Hooker testified he was the only man in the North who could whip General Lee, and that if he had command of the Army of the Potomac, he would march rough-shod over Lee, and take Richmond without any difficulty. He would have got there, too, as a prisoner of war, but for that lamentable occurrence, the accidental shooting, by our own men, of that hero of the war, Stonewall Jackson. Everything being ready with the enemy for an advance, pontoons were thrown across the river, the Yankee army crossed, and our batteries opened on them. The river was filled with killed and wounded; large numbers were drowned. Three times they attempted to cross before they succeeded; then ensued the bloody battle of Chancellorsville, which my reader is perfectly familiar with, and in which that great Napoleon of the war, Thomas Jonathan Jackson, fell by the hand of his own men, and in that fall the star of the Confederacy began to wane, and finally set to rise no more, at Appomattox Court House, Va., on the 6th of April, 1865.

His biographers will do more justice to him than I can; but had he not fallen that night, General Hooker's whole army would have surrendered the next morning or been killed. However, so far, it had been a most complete victory. The enemy lost over thirty thousand, killed, wounded, and prisoners. The news of Jackson's being wounded spread rapidly through the army, and so great was the confidence of the army, and the respect of the commanding general (Lee) for him, that the battle was not renewed the next morning. Hooker's generals declining to lead their men into such slaughter-pens another day, recrossed the Rappahannock the next day with his whole army. Jackson lingered only a few days, and when he passed from this earth there was one universal shriek throughout the land. His death sounded in the ears of the Southerners like the death-knell of the Confederacy. His remains were brought to Richmond on a special train, carried to the Governor's mansion, and there embalmed the next day. The most imposing and the largest procession, military and civil, ever seen in Richmond, bore the body to the Capitol, where it lay in state until the next morning. All the departments of the Government were closed, and business entirely suspended, and bells tolled while the procession was moving. It was indeed a melancholy sight to see the thousands of old men, women, and even soldiers, as the coffin passed into the hearse, drop the tears of sorrow as if some dear member of their family had died. The procession consisted of part of General Pickett's division of veterans, artillery and cavalry and citizens, together with the President and members of the Cabinet. During that afternoon some thirty thousand persons passed in single file the metallic car to get a last farewell glimpse of the features of him who only a few hours before had made the North tremble and the world gaze with wonder and delight at his deeds of valor.

CHAPTER VII.

LEE'S INVASION OF THE NORTH — MOSBY'S CAPTURE OF GENERAL STOUGHTON — THE CONFEDERATE SOLDIER FROM NEW ENGLAND — GENERAL ORDER BY GENERAL STUART — CAPTURE OF WAGONS, ETC. — REMARKABLE ESCAPE OF MOSBY.

THE result of the battle of Chancellorsville again produced the greatest excitement and alarm in Washington. A new draft was ordered, from apprehension of an invasion by Lee. Hooker's army having been nearly destroyed in the Wilderness and Chancellorsville battles, there was nothing in his way to prevent Lee from going into Pennsylvania. He accordingly began to recruit and marshal his forces for an invasion of the North when the season opened. Mosby, who had been sent to the Fauquier Valley, had performed prodigies. Touching his capture of General Stoughton at Fairfax Court House, he thus wrote to a friend in Richmond : —

"You have already seen something in the

newspapers of my recent raid on the Yankees, though I see they all call me Moseley instead of Mosby. I had only twenty men under my command. I penetrated about ten miles in their lines, rode right up to the general's headquarters surrounded by infantry, artillery, and cavalry, took him out of his bed, and brought him off. I walked into his room with two of my men, and shaking him in bed, said, '*General, get up.*' He rose up; and, rubbing his eyes, asked what was the meaning of all this. I replied, '*It means, sir, that Stuart's cavalry are in possession of this place, and you are a prisoner.*' We also surrounded the headquarters of Colonel Wyndham, acting brigadier-general of cavalry, but unfortunately he had gone to Washington. We got his assistant adjutant-general, and also his aid, an Austrian, Baron Woodsan. There was an immense amount of all kinds of stores collected there, but I was unable to destroy them. * * * It was my intention and desire to reach the Court House by twelve o'clock that night, but it being very dark we lost our way, thereby losing two hours. I did not stay in the place more than one hour. On our return to Fauquier, we passed within two hundred yards of the fortifications at Centreville. We were hailed by the sentinel. One of the prisoners, Captain Barker of New York, tried to escape by making a break for the picket, but a pistol-shot from one of the party brought him back. In the vicinity of Fairfax Court House were encamped our cavalry and our infantry brigade. We easily captured the guards around the town, as they never dreamed we were anybody but Yankees until they saw pistols pointed at their heads, with a demand to surrender."

The scout on this raid was a New Englander, — a native of the State of Maine, and a member of the Fifth New York Cavalry, who fought with distinction under the Stars and Stripes. On the proclamation of Abraham Lincoln, liberating the negroes, and the inauguration of drafting men for the army, he refused to serve their cause any longer. He was as fine a specimen of a man as I ever saw. Powerful in frame, a splendid swordsman, and good shot, he was eminent in bravery and courage. He, however, could not fight for the eternal negro. He took French leave of them, and came over and offered his services to Mosby. Mosby was a little shy of him at first, fearing some trap had been set to catch him, and the Yankees sent Ames over to be the instrument in accomplishing it. So he declined to take him at first, but gave him authority to prove the sincerity of his intentions. Ames went out and entered the enemy's camps in the night-time, gained important information, and returned the next morning with two or three horses and prisoners. It was on one of these expeditions that he determined to capture his general. Mosby being convinced by these acts that he was all right, " took him to his bosom." Ames being perfectly familiar with all the picket-posts, the position and strength of the troops at Fairfax Court House, and the unguarded points, Mosby took him on this raid, and the capture was made without firing a shot. After this, he enjoyed Mosby's fullest confidence, and was taken by him on his most perilous expeditions. The boldness and success of this enterprise attracted the attention not only of the whole South and the army, but elicited from General Stuart the following flattering order : —

HEADQUARTERS CAVALRY DIVISION,
March 12, 1863.

GENERAL ORDERS.

Captain John S. Mosby has for a long time attracted the attention of his generals by his boldness, skill, and success, so signally displayed in his numerous forays upon the invaders of his native soil.

None know his daring enterprise and dashing heroism better than those foul invaders, those strangers themselves to such noble traits.

His last brilliant exploit — the capture of Brigadier-General Stoughton, U. S. A., two captains, and thirty other prisoners, together with their arms, equipments, and fifty-eight horses — justifies this recognition in General Orders. This feat, unparalleled in the war, was performed in the midst of the enemy's troops, at Fairfax Court House, without loss or injury.

The gallant band of Captain Mosby shares his glory, as they did the danger of this enterprise, and are worthy of such a leader.

J. E. B. STUART, *Major-General Commanding*.

This bold enterprise stamped Mosby at once as another rising military character, and in due course of time to rank with Stuart, Morgan, Forrest, and the eminent cavalry leaders. As an appreciation of this piece of service, he was promoted to a majority, and designated his battalion as the 43rd Virginia Battalion of Cavalry.

On the 22d of March, 1863, Mosby, with thirty men, attacked the enemy at Bristow Station, on the Orange and Alexandria Railroad. He captured four commissioned officers and twenty-one privates without receiving the least injury. But, owing to the difficulty of getting out, he paroled the privates, and brought off only the officers, who were sent to Richmond. In the spring of 1863, we find Lee on the banks of the Rappahannock, preparing his army for the invasion of the enemy's own country. Mosby, with his headquarters in Fauquier County, was harassing the enemy around Washington, Alexandria, and the line of the Baltimore and Ohio Railroad. He had men with him peculiarly fitted for that kind of service, men remarkable for their courage and acuteness. There were amongst them three brothers from Fairfax County, who served with him in the regular service, and John Bush and Sam Underwood. These boys used to live in the Yankee camps, and always had plenty of greenbacks. John, one night, while scouting between Fairfax and Alexandria, had a cow-bell around his neck, and went into their camp on all-fours, and brought out five of the finest horses he could find, all belonging to officers. Morning came; and the horses were missed, and could be found nowhere. Upon inquiry, and investigating the matter, to their mortification they found they had been duped, which so provoked them that the commanding officer ordered the bells to be taken off every cow in the neighborhood for ten miles around. Poor fellow! he lost his life by bushwhackers while on one of these expeditions near Alexandria.

In April, 1863, when scouting with ten men, and near Centreville, he heard of a wagon-train passing up to the army at Warrenton. He rode into the town in the night-time, and reported to the commanding officer as being in charge of a squad of men sent to guard the wagon-train. The officer in command put Mosby and his squad to guard the rear of the train, which they did successfully; but, when beyond their pickets, the ten rear wagons were ordered to be driven in the woods by the road, and then the horses (forty) were detached from them and carried back to Fauquier. A few days after this, with twenty-five men, he captured, below Billy Goodwin's tavern on the turnpike, forty loaded sutler-wagons. The contents were destroyed; but the horses and prisoners were brought off safely. Early in the month of May, Mosby performed one of the most extraordinary deeds of his whole career. Passing through Prince William County, he and his men, sixty in all, were feeding their horses in the barn-lot of a farm near Dranesville, with saddles off and the gate closed. The Fifth New York Cavalry, two hundred and fifty strong, charged on them with sabres and carbines. Our men took shelter in the barn until twenty-five of them could bridle and saddle their horses; some, including Mosby, mounting their horses bareback, and opening the gate under a heavy fire, charged the enemy with pistols. Our men closed in on them, pouring a deadly fire into their ranks; indeed, every shot seemed to tell. The enemy could not stand such a fire: they broke, and fled in great confusion. We captured seventy horses and twenty-five prisoners, besides killing and wounding about the same number. Mosby and his men sustained neither loss nor injury.

In the month of May, Mosby, with thirty-five men and one piece of artillery, attacked a train of cars on the Orange and Alexandria Railroad, at Warrenton Junction. The guard to the train was driven away and the cars destroyed, and he began to retire. The enemy being reënforced by a regiment of cavalry, pursued him. With this small body of men he fought and kept at bay, for over one hour, the whole regiment of cavalry, and then did not *take care of themselves* until his ammunition was exhausted and artillery captured, and in the retreat he lost only three men, who were captured. A few days after this, when Mosby was returning from scouting in the lower part of Fairfax County, he reached the Bull Run Mountains, and, feeling fatigued, lay down in the shade of one of the large chestnut-trees, and dropped to sleep. While in that condition two Yankees passing by recognized him. They demanded his surrender. Realizing his critical situation, and knowing it would require a bold and sudden movement on his part to extricate himself, and never losing his presence of mind or expressing, in the least degree, excitement under the trying circumstances, he suddenly jumped up, and with one arm, knocked away the pistols pointed at his breast, while, with the other hand, he shot one of his would-be capturers, and the other ran away.

On another occasion during this month, while scouting with Ames, he was, during Ames's absence for a few moments, attacked by *seven* Yankees. Three Yankees were killed, and both parties having exhausted the loads in their pistols, Mosby's adversaries drew their sabres and attacked him. He was as skilful in warding off their thrusts with the pistol as an experienced swordsman, although he had never had a sabre in his hand before this war; besides, he never was partial to the use of this weapon, relying entirely on the pistol. Ames, hearing the firing, came up to Mosby's assistance and saved his life. Ames, being skilled in the use of the sabre, made two of the enemy bite the dust with his sabre, while the other two fled for their lives; and thus was Mosby's life spared to again carry terror into the armies of the invaders of his native soil. Ames himself, in a few days, was placed in a similar situation. He was the bravest Yankee any of us had ever seen. Having determined, when he cast his fortunes with us, to never surrender or be taken alive, my readers can form some idea of the desperation with which he fought when he encountered five of the enemy. It happened in one of the gorges of the Bull Run Mountains, and the scenery and incidents would furnish a splendid theme for the dramatist for a tragedy. In a deep ravine, with a large, ugly rock projecting almost over the pass, surrounded with lofty trees &c., were five men against one, engaged in deadly combat. The one fighting for his life and a great, noble principle, and the other five fighting for a tyrant, plunder, and lucre. Ames emptied his two pistols (twelve loads,) killing two of his adversaries, and repulsing, or rather putting to flight the other three. He himself, however, was severely wounded in the right arm, which rendered him unable to do duty for nearly a year.

CHAPTER VIII.

LEE'S MARCH INTO PENNSYLVANIA—THE CONDUCT OF HIS ARMY CONTRASTED WITH THAT OF THE FEDERALS—BATTLE OF GETTYSBURG—MOSBY ACTIVE—EXTRACT FROM A MONROE, OHIO, PAPER.

IN Richmond, and throughout the South, important and beneficial results were expected from General Lee's invasion of the North. His army was as large as it ever was. The soldiers, flushed with victory, were in splendid spirits. Great and numerous were the speculations in regard to results of the invasion. He began to advance in the month of June, and met with no opposition until the Potomac was crossed. In fact the enemy were ignorant of his whereabouts until the appearance of his troops on the Maryland side of the classic Potomac. His advance guard penetrated the North as far as York, Pennsylvania. Great excitement prevailed in Philadelphia, and serious apprehension was felt that he would attack that city. In Lee's line of march the utmost respect was paid to private property. No private houses were searched for *arms;* no ladies insulted or robbed; no ladies' wardrobes broken open, and robbed of their clothing and jewelry.

How different were the marches of Generals Lee and Stuart, through Pennsylvania and Maryland, from that of General Sheridan's cavalry and the Army of the Potomac, when ladies were insulted and robbed of their jewelry, rings taken from their fingers by force, their entire wardrobes and bed-clothing taken and sent to families in the Northern States! Hen and turkey roosts were robbed; meat-houses broken open and meat taken, leaving not a single piece for the already ruined people; hogs shot down in the fields; sheep and cows driven off; and houses searched, for arms, they said, but in reality for nothing else than for money, jewelry, and fine clothing. Even the poor negro, for whom they expressed so much sympathy, and for whom they were fighting, had his little cabin searched and robbed of what little money he had laid aside for a " *wet day.*"

Milk-houses were broken open and robbed of their contents, and barns and stables burned.

As an instance, when Custer's cavalry were applying the torch to every barn and stable, every rick of hay, wheat, and straw in Loudon County, Virginia, a party of them, led by a major (I regret his name is not known), rode up to a house occupied by a widow lady and daughter, and asked for some refreshments. There was nothing on the place but a very fine spring. After water from that had been furnished, the major ordered his men to apply the torch to the barn and granary. The daughter, a beautiful girl of sixteen summers, came out, and pleaded with the commanding officer (this major) to spare them, declaring no soldiers had ever boarded at her mother's house. He finally consented to spare them at the sacrifice of her virtue. The daughter returned to the house weeping, and this soldier had all the out-houses burned. If this single act is not sufficient to damn the Yankee cavalry in the eyes of the world, it is difficult to say what is so.

Where is that proud spirit of the North, with all its boasted philanthropy; those who profess a sort of Puritanical, par-excellent infallibility; the vicegerents of high Heaven to teach morality? Do they endorse a wholesale war upon defenceless women and children by such vandals? Alas! the human soul shudders at the conviction that these men, by such acts of oppression, were representing a faction who controlled the ship of state at Washington, and expressly obeyed the outside pressure, while those in authority secretly gloated over such outrages. They all loved the Union, *per se*, just as much as William Lloyd Garrison did. He was one of their leaders, and enunciated, as a sort of truism, that "THIS UNION IS A LIE! THE AMERICAN UNION IS AN IMPOSTURE, A COVENANT WITH DEATH, AND AN AGREEMENT WITH HELL! * * * I AM FOR ITS OVERTHROW! * * * Up with the flag of DISUNION, that we may have a free and glorious Republic of our own; and when the hour shall come, the hour will have arrived that shall witness the overthrow of slavery."

In this connection it may not be improper to refer to the numerous arbitrary arrests of non-combatants, by *lettres de cachet*, in other portions of the country, as early as 1862, in verification of our position, that the dominant party in the North really detest the fundamental principles of self-government.

We take the following from the *Congressional Globe*. It relates to proceedings in the United States Senate: —

"Mr. Powell. — I will take this occasion to say what I was about to say a moment ago, when I was held not to be in order. It is not my purpose to enter again into a debate on this subject; but it has been intimated that the remarks I made in regard to the Secretary of State were rather harsh. I admit that they were a little harsh, sir, but I verily believe they were true. I hold in my hand a letter written to me by a very distinguished gentleman of Kentucky, in which he recites an interview that took place with the Secretary of State concerning one of the prisoners from Kentucky, as given to him by Colonel Throop, a gentleman of very high standing, and I beg to read to the Senate an abstract from that letter: —

"'While Colonel Stanton, of this city, was still a prisoner at Fort Lafayette, his brother-in-law, Colonel Throop, employed (through my agency) Mr. Charles F. Mitchell, of Flemingsburg, formerly a member of Congress from New York, and, as I knew, an intimate friend and correspondent of Seward's, to accompany him (Throop) to Washington, to promote Colonel Stanton's release. They were joined at Washington by Frederick Stanton, a brother of Colonel Stanton. The three called on Mr. Seward, Throop and Stanton being introduced by Mitchell. They opened their mission by remarking that they had called to see him in reference to the Maysville prisoners. He abruptly replied that those prisoners would not be released. Frederick asked, "What are the charges against my brother?" Mr. Seward replied, "There are no charges against him on file;" and added that the business of his office pressed him too much to entertain inquiries or give explanations. One inquired if it was his purpose to keep citizens imprisoned, against whom no charges were made. He answered, harshly, "I do not care a d—n whether they are guilty or innocent. I saved Maryland by similar arrests, and so I mean to hold Kentucky." To this it was remarked that the Legislature and public sentiment of Kentucky were averse to such arrests. "I do not care a d—n for the opinion of Kentucky," he insultingly responded; adding that what he required was to hold her in the Union and make her fight for it; and then turning fiercely on Mitchell, demanded of him, "Why the hell are you not at home fighting traitors instead of seeking their release here?" This is the substance of the interview as related to me by Colonel Throop.'

"I will say to the Senate that Mr. Frederick Stanton told me, a few days after it occurred, this very conversation, I will not say in these exact words, but in substance; and I know Colonel Throop to be as honorable a gentleman as lives in Kentucky or any other State."

But I am digressing. We left General Lee on the north side of the Potomac River, advancing into Pennsylvania, — the last intelligence the authorities in Richmond had received of his whereabouts. Ewell was in York, Pa. His extensive line of communication being interrupted, nothing concerning his movements could be heard, except through Northern papers, and they not reliable. There was no uneasiness, however, amongst the people. They knew there was at the head of that army the greatest military chieftain of the nineteenth century. The confidence of the Southern people in him was the same as that which their forefathers reposed in the father of his country in the first revolution. The battle of Gettysburg was fought, and the enemy whipped, as the people of the North know. If they were not, why did they begin to retreat *nine hours* before General Lee? After long marching in the heat of summer, and the men exhausted fighting for several days, with nearly three hundred miles of communication to be kept open, out of ammunition, could a skilful General like Lee commence a pursuit of these who were supplied with abundance of ammunition, particularly when the odds were so great against him, and the enemy receiving reënforcements every hour by their railways? General Lee had (it is estimated) about ninety thousand men in the series of engagements, while the enemy, independent of the army proper, which was estimated at two hundred and fifty or three hundred thousand, had the militia of Pennsylvania, Maryland, New Jersey, New York, and other States of the North. General Lee fell back to Hagerstown near his supplies, and waited there with his men drawn up in line of battle for three days, courting an attack from his adversary, General Meade.

Lee in the meanwhile was not idle. Fortifying himself at this place, he began to recross the Potomac, sending his trains first. If General Lee was whipped as badly as the *Baltimore American* said he was, " his army scattered to the four winds of the heavens and forty thousand of them prisoners," why did not General Meade attack him at Hagerstown, Maryland? Meade knew with whom he was dealing, and, like an able general, declined making such a dangerous and rash movement, notwithstanding the importunities of Stanton. The crossing was effected by Lee without opposition, and he moved thence toward his old position on the Rapidan.

The extravagant and studied falsehoods of the Northern press eventually induced the rulers to believe that Lee's army was very much crippled. The enemy threw a corps forward to annihilate Longstreet. The forces met between Linden and Chester Gaps, in the Blue Ridge Mountains. Longstreet was prepared to meet the attack. Their attempt to dislodge him only served to teach the invaders that the Hills were too steep, Streets too long, and Stonewalls impregnable. The dashing Stewart, with his invincible cavaliers, found work for his arm of the service on the road from Leesburg to Paris. In these engagements and skirmishes the enemy's loss in killed, wounded, and prisoners, was acknowledged to be twelve hundred.

In this memorable campaign Mosby and his partisans were by no means idle. General Lee relied upon this branch of his army for much valuable information as to the disposition and movements of the enemy's forces. His dashes into their lines will doubtless be remembered.

Lee's orders for the preservation of private property, and the protection of professed noncombatants was the subject of some censure.

He had passed over the rich valleys of his native State,— on every hand were the marks of desolation inflicted by a relentless foe,— and marched with a half-naked, shoeless, and starving army, into the enemy's territory teeming with wealth; and notwithstanding the terrible examples set before him, upon his arrival in the enemy's country, no supplies were appropriated without an adequate return of the *quid pro quo*.

In reference to Mosby, who had been denounced by the Yankee scribblers with such select, choice, and classic appellations as " Land Pirate," " Horse Thief," " Murderer," " Guerilla," &c., he strictly refrained from executing the *lex talionis*. His loss during the campaign was one man severely wounded (Alfred Glasscock). To mark the contrast between our mode of conducting the war and that of our enemies, we will here give some extracts from a letter of a private soldier in the Thirty-sixth Ohio Regiment, U. S., published in the Monroe, Ohio, *Spirit of the Democracy* :—

"On the evening of the 11th, five companies of the regiment started on a scout. I set fire myself to several barns, haystacks, straw-ricks, &c. It was pitiful to hear the pleadings of the wives of 'secesh' soldiers, not to destroy their property. We shot all the sheep, pigs, and calves that we could not carry off. In one or two places we came across some bee-hives, and then the men would pitch in and surfeit themselves on the sweet contents. The captain, at one place, sent me down to a house with three men, with orders to search the house, fire the out-houses, and bring off all the cattle that were fat enough to kill. I got the woman to talking with one of the men, and, seizing a brand from the fireplace, set a barn full of wheat afire. I took off two horses, but left her three lean cows. There was a hive full of beautiful white honey, which the men opened, though they were already surfeited. If she had not been a widow, it would have been my duty to shoot the cows, calves and sheep, and leave them to rot upon the ground, if I could not drive them off.

"At the place where we stayed over night, there were two barns full of hay and grain, two haystacks, two straw-ricks, and a large shed burning at once. A grand spectacle! But it made me feel sort of sneaking to destroy property in that way, when there was none to defend it. At two or three places where we burned property the women thought that I was an officer, and came to me and plead for an only cow or an old family horse, and when I referred them to the captain, upon whom they had already exhausted their entreaties, they begged me to use my influence to have them left. One kind-looking woman, whose barn had been set on fire, came to me while I had stopped a moment to fix my accoutrements, after the rest of the company had gone after her cattle, and offered to do anything in the world for me if I would only use my influence to have her cattle left. But I had to hurry off, thinking, as I did so, what I would do to an enemy that would treat my mother and sisters in that way. Would that the vengeance could descend upon the heads of those men who left their families to the mercy of an invader!"

Alfred Glasscock, one of Mosby's most valuable men, was seriously wounded.

CHAPTER IX.

FEELING OF THE SOUTHERN PEOPLE—RECRUITING—THE WRITER JOINS MOSBY—ADVENTURES ON THE WAY—MOSBY'S APPEARANCE.

GENERAL LEE'S return to his old position, somewhat disappointed the people in the South; but when they reflected what long marches his men had made, what a long line of communication he had to keep open, how the enemy were whipped and slaughtered at Gettysburg, how he regained and reoccupied his old position, and stood as proud and defiant as ever, they became satisfied. Appeals were made to the people to come forward and volunteer. The Conscript Act was enforced with more vigor than ever. Young men, with sinecure positions in the departments, resigned and entered the army. Every able-bodied and patriotic young man manifested a desire to have his name associated in some way with the Army of Northern Virginia. Mosby's name by his heroic deeds had become a household word by this time, and all the daring young spirits were eager to join him. Of the regular service they had a holy horror. They imagined if they could only get with Gilman, Imboden, White, or Mosby, they would have an opportunity for active service, could win laurels more lasting, and, if they fell, they would have a resting-place in fame's eternal camping-ground. But the Government at Richmond strictly prohibited all persons liable to military duty from passing through the Confederate lines. Many lily-livered gentry, however, to escape service, flanked our pickets in the night-time, went to the enemy, took the oath, and remained North during the war. The cost of living by this time was exorbitant in Richmond, and the salaries of the clerks in the Departments were utterly inadequate to support them Having read with rapture of Mosby's exploits and deeds of daring, I resolved to resign my position in the Bank of the Confederate States, and cast my fortunes with him for weal or woe. My country and native State needed men in the field, and I felt it a duty to respond to her call, to the extent of my ability.

The restrictions I have just spoken of did not attach to me. By reason of the date of appointment to office, I was at liberty to attach myself to any command. Mosby had returned from Pennsylvania, and established his headquarters in Fauquier County; and, for the distinguished service he had rendered while there, had been promoted to a majority with authority to raise a battalion. Accordingly, Lieutenant Thomas Turner, of Prince George County, Maryland, and Grafton Carlisle, of Baltimore City, were sent to Richmond to get twenty recruits. They took rooms at the Spottswood Hotel, and opened their recruiting office. The first day, before noon, they had over one hundred applications. This number was more than they wanted. I was one of the lucky ones, and resigned my office that day.

Next morning, being the holy Sabbath, I sallied forth to join Mosby, accompanied by several friends on a similar mission. Our route was *via* Virginia Central Railroad, hence to Culpepper, which place we reached

SAM ALEXANDER.

at noon. Culpepper was one of the most delightful towns in the State of Virginia before the war. Some of the noblest specimens of the human race hail from this ancient town. It was then occupied by our cavalry, and General Stuart had his headquarters at Brandy Station, some seven miles distant. We remained here until Turner could go to headquarters, and get passes to carry us through our lines. About three o'clock he returned with passes. The remainder of the Sabbath was spent in travelling to "Old Church," at which point our party of amateurs initiated themselves into soldiers' life, by reclining upon mother earth, and courting "tired nature's sweet restorer, balmy sleep," under the soothing rays of the silver moon. Next morning, after arranging our toilet, an aching void convinced us that we had been fasting twenty-four hours. Our march, however, was resumed, while hunger with its thousand suggestions, forced one of the boys to descry a fair specimen of the swine, which was surrounded; the butcher and cook performed their service with dispatch, and we were served with roast pork, smoked pork.

broiled pork, tenderloin, chine and spare-ribs, minus pepper, salt, or bread.

At the residence of Mr. Rice we were refreshed with a cup of cool, fresh buttermilk. Passing hence we reached Woodson about noon, and bivouacked near Washington, Rappahannock County, the second night. Tuesday our aquatic natures were thoroughly tested by fording, wading, and swimming the Rappahannock River some six times, which contributed to produce our quiet rest on *terra firma*, near the house of John D. Butts, Esq. Being in our novitiate, we were by this time impressed with the conviction that the life of a scout was a dreadful reality. Wednesday morning we were furnished *ex gratia* with a " square meal," so called in military parlance, and reached the place of rendezvous at Markham's, and were allowed to slumber upon the easy side of an oak board in the depot. A relative of Chief Justice Marshall furnished food for twelve of our adventurers, and others ordered breakfast with different families in the vicinity, with as much coolness as though they were *ipso facto* patriots so-called. We were advised that Mosby was making a fashionable call at Scufflebarg, on professional business. During the day we were presented to the illustrious little chieftain; and our first impulse on meeting him was, that—

> "Ours were no hirelings trained to fight,
> With cymbal and clarion glittering and bright;
> No prancing of chargers, no martial display
> No war-trump is heard from our silent array."

Mosby was plainly yet neatly clad in Kentucky jeans, and sat quietly picking his dental plugs with a jack-knife. His carriage is active, easy, and graceful; his affable, genial manners are calculated to win favorable impressions. In speech, he is somewhat taciturn; but his words roll forth with a gentle fluency and decision, and reach the ear in mellow cadence. He is about five feet high, features indicate weight of character and firmness, an honest face, sharp, blue eyes, aquiline nose, light hair, and prominent forehead. In a word, Mosby possesses innate, refined, and exalted sensibilities, and is, by cultivation and education, an elegant, polished gentleman.

August, 1863, Mosby with thirty men went on a raid to Fairfax County. When he got near Billy Goodwin's tavern, on the turnpike below the Court House, he met thirty cavalry leading one hundred horses up to the army. He divided his men to attack them in rear and front,— Lieutenant Thomas Turner, in command of fifteen, to make the attack on the rear, and Mosby with fifteen, attacked in front. The enemy, seeing themselves attacked in that way, broke and took shelter in Goodwin's Tavern, and fired on us from the windows. They, however, after exhausting their ammunition, surrendered. In the engagement the gallant Mosby was wounded in the groin, and calf of the leg. Joe Calvert was wounded in the ankle, and Norman Smith killed. In this gallant young man, Mosby lost one of his most efficient men. He had rendered distinguished service under General Ewell, and was as brave a soldier as ever drew a sabre, and a splendid scout. He was a native of Fauquier County, son of Blackwell Smith (who was a lineal descendant of John Smith), and lived near Warrenton. The enemy lost heavily in this affair. Seventy horses were brought off safe to Upperville, where the recruits were mounted, and the rest distributed among the captors. Mosby's wounds being of a serious character, and there being great difficulty in getting those little delicacies so necessary for the wounded, the Surgeon of the command, Doctor Dunn, advised his removal inside our lines. The day after, he was started in an ambulance to Amherst County, the home of his parents; the command accompanying him as a body-guard as far as Little Washington, in Rappahannock County. During the Major's absence little was done. Lieutenants Smith and Turner directed the new beginners to secure permanent boarding-houses. W. B. Walston, John W. Corbin, John Dickson, Sewall Williams, and myself secured board at Mr. George Short's, and the rest around Paris and Upperville.

The enemy being so near us, we were always on the *qui vive*, and private scouting expeditions were exceedingly popular. Those not mounted would take shot-guns, and go in parties of from five to ten, to Barber's Cross Roads, and capture the enemy's pickets. Lieutenant William R. Smith, of the famous Black Horse Cavalry, but on detached service with Major Mosby on his special requisition, to whom Mosby assigned his men when he left, ordered twenty-five men to meet him at Rector's Cross Roads. Lieutenant Thomas Turner accompanied him. The party proceeded to Waterloo in the night, and attacked the picket at that place, at three o'clock A. M. The picket was composed of " Black Dutch," and easily broken without loss or injury. Twenty-five horses were brought off, with six prisoners. The enemy had five or six killed. Their new clothing, having been drawn the day before the attack, of course fell into our hands.

A few days after this affair, Lieutenant William R. Smith, in conjunction with Lieutenant Turner, took thirty men to Fayetteville, Fauquier County, a little village near Warrenton, to capture a large sutler-store. The Yankee army was on the move; and Smith, with two men, entered Warrenton in the night, with the view of finding out the object of the move. Finding it to be nothing but a feint, he rode up to the column of Yankee cavalry just passing out of the city, and held a little *téte-à-téte* for a few moments, and retired. He then returned to his men, whom he had concealed in the woods, and proceeded with them to Fayetteville to capture the sutler-store. On reaching the store Smith found the proprietor ready to follow the army next morning. The old Jew had in readiness, specially for us, four large four-horse wagons to receive his goods. The Provost Marshal of the army had generously given him a guard of eight infantry, but they, like all regulars, thinking they had a *soft thing* were inside the house playing cards and drinking the old sutler's champagne. The night was very dark. Smith and John Purryear rode up to the door, and knocked. One of the guard thoughtlessly opened the door, when he was politely requested to surrender and keep quiet. In a moment the old Jew was at the door sporting his fine watch and chain, with several diamond rings on his fingers. In the meanwhile the rest of Smith's men came, and soon relieved him of his surplus jewelry and greenbacks, and secured the rest of the safeguard. Then commenced a general ransacking for clothing and other necessaries of life. I will leave my readers to conclude what thirty soldiers would do turned loose into four large rooms, filled up to the very ceiling with every conceivable thing. The men brought their *sacks* into requisition, and filled them. One of them, John ——, of Maryland, found a tin box containing $1,500 in greenbacks. Sixteen fine horses and three prisoners were taken off, the safeguard being set at liberty when we left. It was a rule with Mosby, his officers and men, never to disturb or detain these safeguards longer than he occupied the property on which they were stationed, which fact becoming known, duty of that nature was eagerly sought for by the Federal soldiers. I will hereafter speak of *some* of the service these safeguards rendered Mosby and his officers while their army was encamped around Warrenton.

CHAPTER X.

MOSBY GAINS IMPORTANT INTELLIGENCE FOR GENERAL LEE—APPEARANCE OF THE BATTLE-FIELD AT MANASSAS—CHARGE UPON A PARTY OF THE ENEMY—CONDUCT OF A NEW RECRUIT—CAPTURE OF WAGONS, ETC.—A VERY SOFT THING IS FOUND TO BE TOO HARD.

THE weather being so intensely warm, nothing was done for a week, when an order was issued for a meeting at Rector's Cross Roads, a small village where the Warrenton and Snickers Gap Road crosses the turnpike from Alexandria to Winchester. Only fifteen or twenty men reported. At two o'clock, no scout reporting, we were disbanded. Owing to Major Mosby's temperate habits, his wounds, though painful, healed rapidly, and he was in his saddle again in three weeks. On resuming command of his battalion, he received a hearty welcome from his men. A meeting was ordered to take place at Rector's Cross Roads. Thirty-five men reported. Mosby took command, and at noon we moved off with the view of tapping the Orange and Alexandria Railroad at Bealton Station. It would be impossible to tell here the route we took to reach it, as on our raids Mosby always avoided the highways, and confined his marches to *by-paths* and through woods and fields. We marched that day and night to within two miles of Bealton, and went into camp in the woods until day, when Mosby, W. R. Smith, and John Edmonds went out to reconnoitre. In a few minutes they returned, with the intelligence that the enemy were too strong for us to do anything. They numbered fifteen hundred infantry and five hundred cavalry. Mosby, however, was amply repaid for his trouble by the information he acquired. He saw the enemy receiving a large number of pontoons to be used in the movement General Meade made the ensuing November, when General Lee handled him so roughly on the Rappahannock. Mosby sent Horace Johnson to General Lee's headquarters with dispatches informing him of the designs of the enemy; and, finding the enemy too strong for him with his small squad of men, he changed his course for Fairfax County. On the march we passed through Grinnage to Buckland, where Mosby detailed twenty men to go with him. The rest of the men he sent back to Fauquier County. The detail consisted for the most part of new recruits.

After enjoying the hospitalities of the citizens of Buckland for half an hour, we received the order to mount our horses, and in a few moments we were moving down the turnpike in the direction of Manassas. Passing through Gainesville, we heard of the enemy's being out on a plundering expedition. Our march was over the second, and part of the first, battle-field of Manassas. On either side of the turnpike were the graves of the dead who fell in this sanguinary battle; some of the bones were exposed to the rays of the burning sun, — tops of trees shot off, — entire absence of fences, — houses riddled with bullets, and nothing left of "*the old stone house*" but the bare walls. Our survey of the field was abruptly terminated by one of the party, exclaiming, "*Yonder they are, Major.*" A halt of course ensued; and Mosby, riding up on a little hill about a hundred yards ahead, saw in the distance a party of about thirty-five of the enemy returning to their camp at Centreville by the Thornton Road, leading ten or fifteen horses which they had taken from the citizens. This Thornton Road intersects the turnpike about three miles from Centreville and just below the old stone house near "*Sudley.*" We concealed ourselves under a small hill while the Major watched the enemy. When they had approached within five hundred yards of us he rode back, put himself at our head, and said to his men, "*Boys, I want you to go right through them.*" The charge was commenced with one of those yells peculiar to us, and which I will leave for some of our Northern friends to conjecture and describe. As soon as we were seen, the enemy, thinking we were charging with sabres (our pistols shone so bright), began to unstrap the Enfield rifles from their saddles, with the intention of getting behind the "*worm*" fence hard by; but, on the first fire from our men, they changed their minds and fled precipitately, their quartermaster taking the lead. To reach the enemy we were compelled to charge across a deep ravine, in crossing which several of our horses fell and slightly injured the riders. This delayed for a few moments our reaching the enemy, and afforded them an opportunity to escape; not, however, before nine of them were captured, with twelve horses. Crossing this ravine, too, had the effect of scattering our men; and some of them, in their eagerness to get horses, became separated entirely from the command.

It was in this affair that one of the new recruits acquired prominence as a soldier. He was riding a very high-spirited and fine cavalry horse, without a curb to his bit. On the commencement of the firing, his horse became excited, and ran away with him. Running into a tree, he threw his rider to the ground, and passed on, leaving him afoot. The spirit of the recruit, however, was not broken. Rising to his feet, he continued his charge on foot, and overhauled a Dutch cavalryman, trying to force his horse over the rail fence. With a pistol at his head he was politely requested to surrender and dismount. The recruit was again soon dashing over the field, and overtook Ab Wren and Walker Whaley converging from the dense pine thicket, leading horses, and in search of the command, which had disappeared. All three of the party being provided each with an extra horse, concluded to return to Fauquier. On their way back they were overtaken by Frank Williams, who had likewise got separated from the command. While crossing Bull Run, they were overtaken by a scouting-party of the enemy. The odds being too great to offer any resistance, a precipitate retreat followed, and Frank Williams's fine horse which he had just captured was mired in the stream, and the rider was compelled to seek the bushes to save himself from being captured. Mosby, after waiting on the field some time for his men to come up, resumed his march, with fifteen men, to Fairfax County, where he captured four sutler-wagons heavily laden with stores of every description. In these two little affairs, twenty-five horses and twelve prisoners were brought out, without loss or serious injury to any of his men.

On the 9th of October, Mosby ordered thirty-five of his men to meet him at Rector's Cross Roads. At noon we moved off in the direction of Fairfax. Mosby alone went ahead, and left us in charge of Lieutenant William R. Smith. The first night out we encamped in a pine forest near Frying-Pan, in Fairfax County, Mosby joining us at eleven o'clock that night. Before day next morning, the major, with John Edmonds, Ames, John W. Munson, and Dorsey Warfield, started out on a scout, and penetrated the enemy's lines as far as Falls Church. Lieutenant Smith and Lieutenant Hunter, fearing the enemy might find out our proximity to them, changed our camp, at sunrise, to a pine forest, with an undergrowth of briars, bamboo, and grape-vines so thick that a rabbit could scarcely pass through. Here we remained until orders to move came from Mosby. In the evening of that day, Johnny Edmonds returned with orders to move that night to a certain point near Guilford. Night approached, and it was cloudy. The men could not imagine how they could get out of such a place in a dark night, on foot, to say nothing of horses. But all relied on Smith. His acquaintance with the country (and there was not a foot of ground between the Blue Ridge Mountains and Washington that he did not know) rendered him peculiarly fitted for this kind of service. At ten o'clock we commenced moving. It was so dark we could not distinguish his fileman riding a white horse. We, however, got out safe, with the exception of the loss of a few hats and some scratched faces, and reached Guilford about one o'clock in the morning. We fed our horses with new corn, and grazed them until before day (Sunday), when we rode to a point on the turnpike within five miles of Alexandria, reaching it at sunrise.

The sun never rose with greater splendor. The air was fresh and bracing, and not a cloud broke the blue sky above. Concealing the men in the dense pine forests, some three hundred yards from the turnpike, Mosby and Walker Whaley stationed themselves behind some ivy bushes on the side of the turnpike, and Lieutenant Smith with John Munson took a similar position higher up. In the distance, towards Alexandria, could be heard the tramp of horses and lumbering of wagons. Mosby, with his keen powers of perception, knew instantly what the noise meant. In a few minutes the advance of the cavalry came in full view, and passed on within twenty steps of where the Major was standing. The main column consisted of three hundred and fifty men. Then came the wagons. This guard being to strong for us to cope with, Mosby let them pass on, and the wagons too. In the train there were seventy-five, and opposite Mosby there was one of those bad places in the turnpike which were very general on public highways in those days, especially those used by the Government wagons. Mosby watched this hole, and knew it would be the means of his making a capture. All the teams passed through with difficulty until the third from the last one reached it; that stalled, and the other two could not pass it. In the meanwhile the column passed on, and got a half-mile ahead before the team got out of it. Just as the last wagon disappeared behind a hill, Mosby and Whaley rode out, and politely requested the drivers to drive their teams after him. They complied readily, and turned off the turnpike into a private road leading into the pines where the men were patiently awaiting the arrival. They met with a cordial reception. The drivers, passengers, and horses were soon taken out of the wagon and sent back farther into the woods, and placed in the custody of Lieutenant Hunter. The teams had hardly stopped when commenced one of the most exciting and amusing scenes ever witnessed by any one. Not waiting to remove the covers off the wagons, Bob Lake and John ——, being the first to mount the wagons, out with their pocket-knives, and soon a crevice was made large enough to admit the head of a person. Insensibly the bodies were drawn in, and nothing was seen but feet projecting. Woollen shirts of every hue and style, oysters, sardines, fruits in cans, sugar, coffee, tea, &c., &c., were found. But the most acceptable of all was one hundred and seventy-five pairs of fine cavalry boots. No three wagons were ever unloaded as quick as they were; and, while this was going on, a whole brigade of cavalry passed, in full view of us, up to the army. A great quantity of necessaries were hid in the bushes, with the view of returning to bring them off. Each man being provided with a sack, and some with two, filled them. The rest that was not hid was scattered over the ground.

Lieutenant Smith, with his party, captured one stray wagon, which was about a mile behind the train, that was loaded with cigars, tobacco, candies, cheeses, sugar, syrups, &c., &c. Mosby, with two men, including myself, went over to see if anything could be brought off. On reaching the point where the wagon was, under a hill on the banks of a small stream, I was placed on picket behind a large tree on the brow of the hill, and about fifty yards from the turnpike, while the party went through the wagon. In a few minutes one Jersey wagon came along. I gave the alarm, and Mosby came up, and we rode out to bring the prize in. On reaching it the Major found an old friend of his, with wife, returning empty from Alexandria, where he had been to get his groceries. He had been refused at Alexandria on account of his Southern sentiments; and Mosby invited him over to help himself, free of charge, which he did cheerfully. Out of this team we appropriated nothing but three boxes of raisins, which were kept for the ensuing winter, for a mammoth plum pudding.

Returning to the command, Mosby moved us some three miles farther into the pines, with the view of surprising a camp of black Dutch cavalry numbering about one hundred and fifty. All preparations having been completed, we only awaited the approach of night to move. The scouts, Charlie Hall and Frank Williams, had returned, after an absence of all day, and represented the camp as a *very soft thing*. But the escaping of a prisoner (Union citizen) induced Mosby to abandon the enterprise for fear he would inform the enemy of our plans. This citizen was a dangerous character, and had on former occasions given the enemy information of our being about. So soon as his escape was known, Mosby abandoned his project for the present, and moved his men back to Loudon County. A division of the plunder was made on the farm of Mr. Kidwell, and the men disbanded, while Mosby, with two men, returned to Fairfax. Our long absence had aroused the most serious apprehensions for our safety. On former raids we had never been absent more than three days at the farthest; but on this we were out six days, and our friends in Fauquier having received no intelligence concerning us during our absence, were apprehensive all were captured. Our return was received with great rejoicing in Fauquier. On this raid not a pistol was fired, while we captured and destroyed seventy-five thousand dollars' worth of property.

CHAPTER XI.

AFFAIR WITH A DETACHMENT OF CAVALRY—CAPTURE OF A WAGON-TRAIN—ORGANIZATION OF ANOTHER COMPANY—FEASTING—ATTACK UPON THE CAMP AT WARRENTON—PRISONERS, ETC., TAKEN.

ON the third day after our return, Mosby ordered a meeting of all the men at Middlebury. The whole Yankee army was on the move; and, if possible, he would capture some of their wagon-trains. The guards, however, were too strong for us to do anything. We then looked out for patrols and scouting-parties. Returning from Fairfax, in Prince William County, we fell in with a detachment of cavalry, and captured twenty horses and the same number of prisoners; also forty mules they were leading to the army. On going through them, we found in their saddle-pockets, sardines, oysters, peaches in cans, &c., which they had got from the wagons abandoned by us one week before. All hands returned home without loss or injury to any one.

One week after this, thirty of the men were taken by the Major to Fairfax. Nothing was accomplished on this occasion except the capturing of six horses and prisoners at Centreville. On the day of our return, a meeting was held at Rectortown, a little village on the Manassas Gap Railroad. There was a full attendance. Mosby made a detail of thirty men with fresh horses, to meet him at sunset in Salem. At dark he moved off in the direction of Warrenton. Leaving that place to his right, he proceeded to New Baltimore, and struck here, before daybreak, a wagon-train, and captured one hundred and fifty mules, forty horses, twenty-five Yankees, and fourteen negroes, and returned the next morning without loss or injury. The appearance of such a large body of mules, horses, &c., produced the greatest excitement along the route of our return. Our friends imagined we were the enemy, and we amused ourselves very much seeing the citizens running off their stock to the woods and mountains. The horses were divided amongst the men. The prisoners, including the negroes, were sent to Richmond, and the mules were sold to the Government. Mosby, being so successful on this raid, concluded to take the whole command down to the same place next day. On reaching New Baltimore, he found he was just one hour too late. A train of over one hundred wagons had passed up without a single guard. We returned next day to Fauquier, and were disbanded until further orders.

The next meeting of the command took place at Scuffleburg, on the 1st day of October, 1863. Scuffleburg is a small village situated about midway on the road between Markham and Paris, in the hollow of the Blue Ridge Mountains, and is a place peculiarly adapted to the meeting of partisan rangers to transact business pertaining to their system of warfare. The buildings of the town consist of one blacksmith-shop with residence attached thereto, and a wheelwright's shop. The enemy had never visited the place. During the years 1863 and 1864, or rather the year after the occupation of Fauquier County by Mosby, it was considered a place of no little importance by the enemy. It was near this place the heroic and lamented

Ashby was born, and over this road that Jackson made some of his celebrated flank movements. It was also considered as the headquarters of the "guerilla Mosby," and a rendezvous of his men. The enemy imagined it a second Gibraltar, filled with all kinds of infernal machines and implements of warfare, and believed that none of them who got there ever returned. The foot of no Yankee soldier ever trod its magnificent thoroughfares, or reposed his wearied form under the stately oaks and chestnuts, from the rays of the burning sun, while the mountain breeze refreshed his burning cheek with the perfume of the wild honeysuckle, and the air was musical with the songs of birds, until General Meade occupied that country on his pursuit of General Lee, after his Pennsylvania campaign.

The meeting on the 1st of October was for the purpose of organizing the second company of the Forty-third Virginia Battalion of Cavalry, Company B. Company A had assumed the proportions of a battalion itself, and Mosby concluded to organize another company. All the men were drawn up in a line, and Mosby selected sixty therefrom, and ordered the men to go into an election of officers. William R. Smith of Fauquier County, in view of the distinguished services he had rendered the Confederacy while a lieutenant of the famous Black Horse Cavalry, — his noble spirit, generous disposition, attachment to the men, and, above all, his daring courage, and extensive knowledge of the country, — was unanimously elected captain of Company B. Frank Williams, of Fairfax, who had, since the commencement of the war, made so many of the enemy bite the dust in his own native country, and was such a terror to them, was elected first lieutenant; and Albert Wren and Bob Grey, who had rendered similar services, were elected second and third lieutenants. Horace Johnson of Warrenton, who had served with Smith in the Black Horse Cavalry, with distinction, was appointed orderly sergeant. After the organization, Captain Smith disbanded us, with orders to meet him the next day at Salem. Forty men reported for duty. At noon we moved in the direction of Warrenton. On the approach of night there was every indication of a storm. The clouds increased in blackness, and the darkness was beyond the power of conception. Indeed, so intense was the darkness, the men could not distinguish their filemen. The rain fell in torrents, and we moved only when we had lightning. At twelve o'clock we reached the home of our captain, and sought shelter in a schoolhouse, some two hundred yards from the house, tying our horses to the trees. The captain's mother and sisters had prepared a sumptuous supper for us, after which, William Chapman and Montjoy sang delightfuly for the ladies. On the break of day we moved back to the mountains and disbanded, with orders to meet at Mr. Cross's, about six miles from Warrenton, punctually, at four o'clock. We scattered over the neighborhood, and were welcomed and hospitably entertained by the farmers. Mr. ——, at whose house myself and friend (Foley Kemper, nephew of General Kemper) were entertained, and his acomplished daughters, and estimable lady, were particularly kind to us. We listened with delight to their performances on the piano, and their singing. And now, at this distant day, when I recall the hours I have spent so happily around the firesides of our friends in that country, in the society of their charming daughters, it seems like a dream. Our high appreciation of those kind offices shown while we were with them, has been sufficiently demonstrated by the protection we afforded them.

Four o'clock came and all hands at Mr. Cross's. Taking a private road we moved towards Warrenton, and reached an old church on the main road, some two and a half miles from Warrenton, about dark. Here we took a stand. Before us could be distinctly seen the signal lights on the cupola of the Court House. Pickets were posted, with orders to allow no one to pass either way. At eleven o'clock we moved off, observing the utmost quiet. Not even a whisper broke the stillness of the night. The night being very dark the town was flanked without discovery. Indeed, so important was it that no noise should be made, that rocky places in by-paths were covered with oil-cloths and blankets to prevent the noise of the tramp of our horses being heard by the enemy. We got three miles in the rear of the town and halted under a high hill, out of view of the enemy's pickets. Captain Smith, William Chapman, and Montjoy went out to ascertain the exact position and strength of the enemy, who were only about one mile distant. They passed all through the enemy's camp on foot, having tied their own horses amongst those of the enemy. They found the capture of the camp a difficult matter, owing to the fact of the number of soldiers being doubled the day before; and, instead of one hundred and twenty-five men, there were two hundred and fifty. In addition to that, their position was a peculiar one. Their camp was on the brow of a hill formed like a horse-shoe. At the base of this hill, or in the bottom, were some apple-trees, to which their horses were tied, while on the slope of the hill were their tents. From the front of their camp or top of the hill, were roads diverging in every direction, and strong pickets posted thereon. In their rear was an open, low country extending for a mile, as it likewise did on both sides, and no pickets posted. A consultation was held as to how the attack should be made. Chapman and Montjoy urged the attack in front to charge the pickets and follow them in. Smith thought otherwise. He determined to attack them with his small squad in the rear.

Their long absence began to excite serious apprehensions as to their safety. Several picket-shots were heard, and it was believed, amongst the men, our raid would be a failure. Finally, about four o'clock in the morning, Smith, Chapman, and Montjoy returned. Diligent inquiries were made of the officers, by the men, as to their intentions. They received the consoling reply: —

"*If you all will go in, there will be a horse for each of you.*"

The order was given to mount, and soon the camp-fires of the enemy were seen in the distance. On approaching nearer, the number of the fires increased. It was about half past four the attack was made. Not expecting a call from the rebels at that hour in the morning, they permitted us to get within ten yards of their fires (around which some of the enemy were sitting) before Captain Smith ordered the charge. The boys gave one of their unearthly yells; and, in an instant, we were in the centre of their camp, firing right and left, dealing death wherever our shots were directed. In the charge of the advance, one voice (Sam A.) could be heard ringing through the air like a clarion voice, "Give me your greenbacks! surrender!" Some of the men charged through the fires. The enemy rallied in a few moments, on the top of the hill, and commenced a charge down on our left flank, firing at the same time several volleys from their carbines. Captain Smith, with his quick powers of perception, seeing the imminent danger of his small band being cut off and probably captured, gave the order to "*bring up the other squadron.*" The enemy, thinking we had a large reserve behind, commenced retreating to the top of the hill, where they contented themselves with firing over our heads. We in the meanwhile secured twenty-seven horses, six prisoners, and one negro, and retreated, under cover of night, without loss or injury to any one, although the Yankee commander of the post reported to the Secretary of War at Washington, "*He was attacked that morning by a body of guerillas. They were repulsed with heavy loss. It is supposed a large number were killed and wounded, as they could be tracked for miles by the blood of their wounded which they carried off with them.*"

CHAPTER XII.

CAPTURE OF TWO CORRESPONDENTS OF THE "NEW YORK HERALD"
— EXPEDITION TO CAPTURE GOVERNOR PIERPONT — RAID TO
BEALTON STATION, ETC.

IN the month of November of this year, 1863, while Mosby was returning from a scout in Fairfax, in passing through the little village of Auburn, he captured two correspondents of the "New York Herald," at Mr. McCormick's. On Mosby's appearance in front of the house, the front door was closed, and admission denied him. An order from him, however, soon opened it. The greatest excitement prevailed amongst the ladies. On tendering the correspondents the contents of two revolvers if they did not surrender, they gracefully complied with the Major's request. The ladies threatened to bring down the displeasure of General Lee on Major Mosby's head if he did not release their friends. Mosby was not a man to be intimidated in that way. He invited them to their horses, which they mounted, and returned with him to Fauquier. There they were furnished with a military escort to Richmond.

A few days after this, Mosby took four picked men on a scouting expedition to Fairfax, with the intention of capturing Governor Pierpont. He penetrated the enemy's lines to the very *gates* of Alexandria. On reaching the house in which he expected to find the Governor, he learned he had left that evening for Washington City. He then proceeded to the house of Colonel Dulaney. Mosby, on entering the house, was met at the door by the colonel. Dulaney expressed delight " at meeting with Jesse scouts," and invited Mosby in, and asked him his business, when to his amazement, French Dulaney, his son, stepped in and invited his father to get on his horse and accompany them to Fauquier and Richmond.

Early in December, Mosby, with seventy men, started on a raid to Bealton Station, on the Orange and Alexandria Railroad. We arrived within three miles of the place the first night, remaining in the woods until daylight, when we moved up the railroad about five miles, and took up a position among some heavy timber, concealing ourselves from the enemy. On each side of us were encamped Gregg's cavalry, while in front, about one mile distant, on a high hill, were the general's headquarters, at which there was a morning's review of the troops. In this position we remained in the rain until noon, watching for a wagon train to return from the depot loaded with supplies for headquarters, when John Munson and Walter Whaley brought in two bluebirds, one walking and the other riding. The one riding was a guard and bearer of dispatches to General Gregg's headquarters; the other afoot was a deserter under sentence of death, and was on his way to be shot. The condemned man was set at liberty on a captured mule, and the bearer of dispatches sent to Richmond. Mosby almost despaired of the wagon-train's returning; while the men, cold, wringing wet, and the rain falling in torrents, thought of returning to Fauquier. At two o'clock those apprehensions were dispelled by the order to "*mount your horses.*" Mosby ordered Captain

Smith to take Company B. and charge the enemy in front, while he took fifteen men of Company A, and attacked them in the rear. He succeeded in cutting off the rear and capturing the whole party, consisting of five wagons loaded with medical stores, and a guard of twenty-five cavalry. By a miscalculation of the distance, Mosby did not strike them until after Smith was in, and then on their flank. Notwithstanding the rain, which fell in torrents, Smith, with Company B, swept down, like a tornado, on the guard which was in the advance. The enemy made not the slightest resistance, not even firing a shot, but wheeled and made for their camp, which was about one mile distant, leaving the wagons and teams a prey to us. Two of the guard, however, were captured, besides eight fine mules and six horses. Mosby sustained no injury whatever. The wagons were loaded with valuable medical stores, and had the capture been anywhere else than in sight of the general's headquarters, they would have been brought off and sent to General Lee. One or two men secured a few valuable articles used in surgery, and turned them over to Dr. Dunn, surgeon of the battalion. The fugitives, having reached camp, reported our audacity; and one regiment of cavalry was sent in pursuit. They pursued us until dark.

Captain Stringfellow, one of General Stuart's scouts, was our scout on this occasion, and, in company with one of our men, stopped at Mr. Skinker's, six miles from Warrenton, under the mountains, to stay all night. The rest of the men had crossed the Bull Run Mountains, and gone into camp at Salem. The enemy, thinking a number of our men would lie over at Mr. Skinker's until next morning, surrounded the house and commenced an indiscriminate firing into the windows and doors, to the great peril of Mr. Skinker's family, calling, during the firing, for Mosby's men to come out. Stringfellow, perceiving no avenue of escaping out of the house, secreted himself in one of those *secret closets* which our Southern friends always had ready for us, and escaped, although the enemy instituted a diligent search. The enemy carried back with them Stringfellow's horse and fine mare, which he had just captured of them; also Mr. Skinker and his son, whom they *robbed* of one thousand six hundred dollars in greenbacks. Mr. S. and son were sent to Warrenton and to Washington.

The next morning, before day, the pursuit was resumed. Taking the road direct to Salem, the enemy dashed in there at early breakfast, and captured two of our men who had been detailed to go out with the prisoners. The sergeant of the guard, Dorsey Warfield, sent our prisoners on to Oak Hill, three miles farther, while he and several of the men stopped there to see their families. It was in Salem, on this occasion, a young man, who will hereafter figure most conspicuously on every raid made by Mosby, exhibited a spirit of coolness and bravery rarely excelled by any one during the whole war, and whose conduct pleased Mosby so much that he made him first lieutenant of Company C. When the enemy dashed into town, very few of the citizens were up; and, before he could dress himself, the place was surrounded, and all avenues of escape closed. Fearing they would spend the day there, he determined, by one bold movement, to free himself. His horse had been taken by the enemy. He buckled on his pistols, and started out afoot, with the determination of fighting his way through them. He managed by adroitness to get some distance from town before discovery. Five cavalrymen charged him and fired. The compliment was returned by him. Being a splendid shot, he made three bite the dust. The other two retreated, and he mounted a Yankee horse and escaped; he receiving in the affray only a slight wound in the hand. This young man was Adolphus E. Richards, of Fauquier County, Virginia, and a minister of the Presbyterian School.

CHAPTER XIII.

MOSBY CAPTURES ONE HUNDRED AND TWENTY MULES AND TEN HORSES FROM A WAGON-TRAIN, BURNING FORTY WAGONS—YANKEES CAPTURED—BOLD EXPLOIT OF MONTJOY.

IN December, 1863, Mosby took the command to Brandy Station on the Orange and Alexandria Railroad. The whole Yankee army was moving on General Lee's lines on the Rappahannock. At the Station, part of General Sedgwick's wagon-train, guarded by a brigade of infantry, was preparing to move. The large camp-fires illuminated the country for miles around. The wagon-master was riding up and down the train, hurriedly urging the teamsters to hurry up, that the rear guard had moved off. Mosby, with two men, rode up to him, and complained about the delay of the train. He also rode through the guard while they stood around the fires with their arms stacked, and conversed with them in regard to the object of the movement of the army. He thus threw the enemy off their guard, representing his cavalry as the last of their rear-guard. Returning to his command he placed himself at their head and moved them quietly to the wagons, which were standing some fifty yards from the fires, and proceeded to detach the mules and horses, and got out one hundred and twenty mules and ten horses before the enemy was aware of what he was doing. The first intimation they had of his doings was seeing the flames issuing from forty wagons which had been set on fire by the last of his men that left the train. Before they could unstack their arms Mosby was out of their reach, with the mules and horses. They, however, fired one volley at him, without inflicting injury upon any one. The mules were sent to General Lee, and the horses divided amongst the men.

Mosby, being so successful on this raid, took both companies to Brandy Station the day after his return, with the hope of getting another train. In the meanwhile General Meade sent two regiments of Rhode Island cavalry back to *protect* the country between the Rappahannock and Hazel rivers. After crossing Hazel River, at sunset, we halted under a hill about half a mile from the Wellford Farmhouse, now owned by a Union citizen of Richmond, to await further orders from Mosby, who had gone ahead of his men with Stringfellow. Not hearing from him by seven o'clock, Lieutenant Thomas Turner, of Company A, moved us up to the Wellford House, and occupied the out-houses which had been used by the enemy as meat-houses. Fires were built in the old-fashioned fireplaces, out of the boxes left by the enemy, and we made ourselves as comfortable as circumstances would permit. At ten o'clock that night, Mosby and Stringfellow returned with two Yankees, belonging, they said, to an Indiana regiment. They were very soon gone through. Mosby captured them while they were out *foraging*. On examining them, papers and books were found which they had stolen from the library of a gentleman (a Mr. Thorn) in Culpepper County, whose house they had plundered and burned, turning the whole family out of doors with only the clothes on their backs, for no other reason than that he was a Southern man. The next morning we recrossed the Hazel River, and lay in the dense pine woods adjoining the farm of Mr. Majors.

Mosby having learned the position of the enemy on the other side of the Hazel River during his absence, sent Lieutenant Thomas Turner, Montjoy, Henry Ashby, and three others out reconnoitring. They recrossed the Hazel, and proceeded to the enemy's camp to see if anything could be done. Turner, concealing his men from the enemy in some bushes near their camp, began, with Montjoy, to dodge around their camp. The Yankees, seeing them, sent one man out to see who they were. He was "gobbled up," and they sent out another who shared a similar fate. Turner and Montjoy then returned to their comrades; and, after a few moments' delay, proceeded to take a picket-post of ten men just as they were being posted some two hundred yards from the camp. The two prisoners fell into line, and accompanied them, riding in front. The weather was intensely cold, and all the party wore blue overcoats (except Turner and Montjoy) to deceive the enemy. Their movements did not attract the attention of the enemy until they were within fifty yards of the picket, when they were halted by the sergeant of the guard with, —

"Halt! who comes there?"

"*Friends*," replied Montjoy.

"What command?" again cries the picket.

"First Maine Cavalry!" responds Montjoy.

"All right, — advance!" cries the picket; and Montjoy moves up by twos to the post, each man passing on either side. After some moments' conversation, Montjoy instructed them to "*keep a sharp lookout for Mosby.*" At a certain signal nearly every picket had a pistol pointed at his head, with the invitation to follow them. Being almost paralyzed by the boldness and audacity of Montjoy's trick in the broad blaze of day (it being about noon), and so near their camps, they complied, without the least show of resistance; and all the post were soon the other side of the Hazel in a safe place. Their capture was soon discovered, and a party started in pursuit. These approached the river cautiously; and, after displaying themselves on the high hills a mile distant from us, they returned to their camps without firing a shot. Montjoy and Turner had only six men with them, and captured twelve prisoners, horses, and accoutrements, without loss or injury. Mosby, coming up in a short time, ordered us to return to Fauquier. The weather being so intensely cold, nothing was done until the 1st day of January, 1864.

CHAPTER XIV.

AFFAIR WITH COLONEL COLE'S CAVALRY—SIXTEEN OUT OF EIGHTY "LEFT TO TELL THE TALE"—CAPTURE OF HORSES, ETC.—EXCESSIVE COLD—SPLENDID SCENE.

THE 1st of January, 1864, was anything but a pleasant day for a soldier. The snow had been on the ground for two weeks, thawing in the daytime and freezing at night, until it was absolutely dangerous to travel on horseback. The last day of the old year, however, was very pleasant; and the snow and ice had disappeared in great measure. The sun on the morning of the new year rose with all the grandeur of which the imagination can conceive. But clouds began soon to cover the sky, and by noon snow was falling. Mosby was absent on a scouting expedition in Fairfax; and Captain Smith had ordered a meeting of the men at Rectortown, with the intention of making a new-year's call on some

Yankee camp. The enemy, however, concluded to save him the trouble; and, accordingly, eighty of Colonel Cole's battalion of *Maryland* cavalry, doing guard duty at Harper's Ferry, dashed into Upperville about eight o'clock A.M., on the 1st day of January, and captured two or three of our men while they were at breakfast. The party was commanded by a Captain Hunter; and, while there, they heard we were to have a meeting at Rectortown at noon. They determined to break it up. Concluding that most of the men were absent at their homes, spending the holidays, no resistance was apprehended. At noon it was snowing; and some ten or twelve had met at Rectortown, awaiting the arrival of Smith. I was at Joe Blackwell's, our headquarters, and had just left Smith with four or five men to attend meeting.

As I was crossing the railroad at Goose Creek, some two miles from the town, three of our men were seen dashing into Goose Creek at full speed. On seeing myself and companion, they exclaimed, "Don't go to Rectortown: it is full of Yankees, and we were run out of the place." I immediately returned to Joe Blackwell's, where I had left

Smith, and reported the fact. He mounted his horse, and bid us follow him. During my absence, eight or ten men had assembled there. We obeyed his order, and pushed on, eager for the prey. Crossing Goose Creek, he carried us to Mrs. Rawling's, at the top of a hill, and told us to remain there until further orders to move; while he, Sam Alexander, and Frank Williams reconnoitred a little to find out the strength of the enemy, their position, &c., &c. The suspense we were in while at Mrs. Rawling's was soon relieved by the appearance of Frank Williams with orders for us to advance. In a few minutes we were in Rectortown, and were joined there by others of the command, which swelled our force to twenty-seven in all. Not tarrying there any time, we dashed on after the enemy. The enemy, in leaving Rectortown, tried to deceive us by taking the Warrenton Road. Keeping that road for one and a half miles, they filed off to the left, and took the road by the Five Points to Middlebury. But the vigilant eye of Smith could not be deceived. While in Rectortown, Smith found out whose command they belonged to, and left orders for us to take the

Five Points Road, near which place he would join us. While following them up, we were joined in Rectortown by others of our command, which swelled the whole to twenty-seven men; and, not stopping in town, we pushed after the enemy. Getting outside of the limits of the town, R. P. Montjoy, Henry Ashby, and John Edmonds, were thrown forward as an advanced guard. Just beyond the Points our advance came upon the rear of the enemy, and shots were exchanged. The enemy had taken a strong position in the road, — on one side of them a high stone wall, while on the other was an open, cleared country, extending almost as far as the eye could reach. So we could take no advantage of them. They had formed in the road, and were awaiting our attack. Smith threw himself at the head of his men, and ordered us to charge, so that we would have the *bulge* on the enemy. At the first fire, Captain Hunter, their commander, had his horse shot under him; and, before waiting to see whether or no rider and horse both were killed, his men were seized with a panic, and broke and fled in every direction. An effort was made to rally them in an open field, on the right of the road: but the gallant Smith would not give them time; our style of fighting being to pitch in, and " clean " the enemy out, or be " cleaned out." In we went, when Hunter's horse fell, and himself was made prisoner. The rest retreated in great confusion, through woods and through marshes, into which some were thrown from their horses head-foremost, and stuck there some ten or fifteen minutes until extricated by some of our men who had charge of the prisoners.

Beyond this marsh, some three hundred yards, was a body of heavy-timbered land, in which a large number took shelter, hoping we would not pursue them. Generally woods do afford great protection from the attacking party; but, in this instance, they sought their own captivity. Back of these woods was a little stream called Carter's Run, very shallow and narrow, while the banks were high. In jumping their horses over this stream, some fifteen or twenty of them were precipitated into it with their horses. Sending these back to the rear, Captain Smith, with Lieutenant Turner, Bush Underwood, and ten others, continued the pursuit as far as Woodgrove, London County. Out of the eighty men

WALTER FRANKLAND.

brought up to "Mosby's Confederacy" by Captain Hunter, to capture Mosby and his men, and present them to Father Abraham as a new-year's gift, sixteen only got back to their camp at Harper's Ferry, to tell the tale. Eight were killed on the field; fifty-four were sent prisoners to Richmond; while the wounded were paroled, and taken by the farmers into their houses, where they received every attention. Sixty fine horses, with equipments, including thirty fine army pistols, were secured and distributed amongst the victors. The sabres and carbines we threw away, as they were weapons we had no use for.

And I will here suggest to the Government agents, now collecting Government arms throughout the different rebel States, that, if they will make a visit to Mosby's battle-fields, they may find several wagon-loads, provided the Freedman's Bureau has not given them to the "colored gemmen." Early in the afternoon the wind shifted around to the north; and, before sunset that day, the mercury was at zero. When we reached Joe Blackwell's with the capture, the feet of our men were frozen to their stirrups; while the prisoners, who had fallen into Carter's Run, were just one sheet of ice, and nearly frozen speechless. Smith had placed the prisoners in my custody until after the division. I moved them, including our men, to the woods on the left of Joe Blackwell's, about one hundred and fifty yards; and ordered them to build large fires, and warm themselves, while we awaited the arrival of Captain Smith, who in a few minutes rode up nearly frozen. In a short time the horses and pistols were soon divided amongst the men, and a detail made to carry out the prisoners. This affair was of such a brilliant character, when we consider the odds against us being nearly four to one, we having nothing but pistols, while the enemy were armed with pistols, sabres, and carbines, all of the most improved kind, elicited from Major Mosby an order of the most flattering character, complimenting Captain Smith and his small band of men in the highest manner for their bravery and success in this affair. It is a source of deep regret I cannot produce the order here to my readers; but it, with all Major Mosby's papers, reports, orders pertaining to the battalion, from General Lee, Stuart, and others, were burnt up with Joe Blackwell's house, in March, 1864.

Colonel Cole met with such a brilliant new-year's reception that he made but one more expedition into "Mosby's Confederacy."

The scenery on the mountains, on the evening of the 1st of January, was of the most sublime character. In the forenoon of the day, a *wet snow* fell, and melted almost as fast as it fell. The air, during the forenoon and middle of the day, was fresh and pleasant; but the winds in the afternoon shifted to the north, and at sunset everything was frozen hard. Not a cloud broke the blue sky above as the sun was setting in the west behind its fiery curtains. The mountains seemed as one vast sheet of ice, and the reflection of the sun's declining rays on the scene was indeed sublime. It was a scene which would have enraptured the artist, and inspired the poet.

CHAPTER XV.

CAPTURE BY LIEUTENANT TURNER AND HIS MEN—MEN FROZEN—CAPTAIN STRINGFELLOW—DARING EXPLOIT.

HEAVY and deep snows fell during this week, and the weather continued intensely cold without intermission; indeed, so severe was the cold that it was a hard matter to get the men to expose themselves at night. Notwithstanding those obstacles, Lieutenant Thomas Turner and Joe Nelson, of Company A, took twenty-five men, on the night of the 4th of January, and proceeded to a point near Warrenton, to capture a patrol of fifty Yankees. The night was one of the coldest ever experienced in that country by the oldest residents. The mercury stood below zero, and snow one foot deep was on the ground. Many of Turner's men had their hands and feet frost-bitten that night, and the hands of all were so benumbed with cold that they could scarcely use their pistols to advantage. The Yankees felt the cold almost as sensibly as Turner's men. To keep comfortable, they would ride up and down the road without dismounting. It was on their return to camp that Turner met this patrol. As I said before, the snow was on the ground some twelve inches deep. Fortunately for Turner, the wind was blowing almost a perfect hurricane, which had the effect of drowning all noise that could be made by another body of cavalry approaching. In fact, so perfectly safe from all attack by "guerillas" did the enemy think themselves that night, that Lieutenant Turner, with his twenty-five men, rode up within *ten feet* of them before they knew we were about, or the charge was ordered by Turner, when a yell and deadly fire was opened on them from the pistols of Turner's men. The surprise was so great and unexpected that not the slightest resistance was offered by the enemy, who begged, for God's sake, that we would not shoot them. Our firing ceased instantly. We "gathered together" *forty-five* horses and twenty-five prisoners, which we brought off safely. The dead and wounded were left on the field. Turner had not a man injured in this affair. However, William B. Walston lost several toes by frost; *General Geary* lost four fingers from one hand; and John W. Corbin, of Accomac County, Virginia, had both hands and feet frozen. With these exceptions, there were no casualties whatever on this raid.

On the 7th day of January, Major Mosby received a note from Captain Stringfellow, written in London County, suggesting his coöperation with him in capturing " Cole's Battalion," doing picket duty on the London Heights, opposite Harper's Ferry, stating that the enemy was picketing only one road,— the turnpike leading to Hillsboro', and that he could take Mosby and his men into their camp, and capture the whole concern without the firing of a shot.

As Stringfellow was the originator of this brilliant and unfortunate foray, I will here give my readers, by way of parenthesis, an idea of who he is and how he happened up there. Captain Stringfellow had entered the Confederate army at the very beginning of the war, and had distinguished himself on numerous battle-fields. Those actions had not passed unobserved by that great cavalier, General J. E. B. Stuart. Stringfellow's thorough knowledge of all that country stretching east of the Blue Ridge Mountains down to the Federal Capital, embracing the counties of Loudon, Fauquier, Prince William, Fairfax, Culpepper, Orange, &c., and his bravery and dashing behavior on the battle-field, as well as the perilous journeys he had performed for his superiors, justly recommended him to Stuart for promotion. Stuart accordingly appointed him captain of his scouts, and gave him ten men to operate with. As he was not regularly attached to the Forty-third, little is known of his general operations. Yet I cannot restrain myself from mentioning several deeds of daring performed by him, which were unparalleled in the history of warfare.

While the Federal army was encamped at Culpepper Court House and Brandy Station, on the Orange and Alexandria Railroad, General Sedgwick, commanding the Sixth Army Corps, established his headquarters at the Wellford House, about two miles from Brandy Station. Stringfellow had been dispatched by General Stuart, to obtain some valuable information from the enemy. The vigilance of the enemy's pickets prevented him from accomplishing his purpose by those means which heretofore had carried him through successfully; and, as a last resort, he adopted the plan of entering the enemy's camp in disguise. Providing himself with a Yankee colonel's outfit, and putting on a bold face, in the broad blaze of day he rode up to the enemy's camp. He was saluted by the pickets, and rode up to General Sedgwick's headquarters. The General, with his staff and one or two guests, was at dinner. Nothing wrong being suspected, he was invited to dismount and share their dinner with them. Stringfellow, having lived so much in the enemy's lines, had made himself familiar with all the enemy's camps, the names of the regiments, their officers, and the position of the troops. Representing himself as colonel of a regiment at the extreme end of their lines, and satisfying the officers that he was all right, Stringfellow was invited into the tent, to be one of the dinner-party. A general conversation ensued, in which he so completely gained the confidence of all around the table, that he not only found out what he was sent to discover, but more too, including the strength of the whole army, their position, and *intentions*. Having accomplished the object of his visit, he remounted his horse, rode through their pickets, and reported to Stuart what he had done.

On another occasion, when on a scouting expedition in the neighborhood of Warrenton, dressed in a Yankee overcoat, five Yankees overtook him on the road. They questioned him critically in regard to the command he belonged to, and being satisfied with his representations, they passed on. When they were some fifteen steps ahead of him, he drew his two pistols and fired away at them. As he was a splendid shot, at the first fire two bit the dust; at the second fire a third one fell, and the other two fled for their lives, without exchanging a shot.

CHAPTER XVI.

PLAY AT ALEXANDRIA, ENTITLED, "THE GUERILLA"—MEETING AT UPPERVILLE — EXPEDITION — PLAN OF CAPTURE — FAILURE OF PLAN — LOSS OF SMITH, TURNER, PAXON, COLSTON, ETC.

IN the spring of 1864, there was a play introduced and performed in the theatre at Alexandria, Virginia, entitled "The Guerilla; or, Mosby in Five Hundred Sutler-wagons." The play of course excited a great deal of attention amongst us, including Mosby himself. Flaming bills were posted all over the city, and a programme was sent to Mosby. The strongest desire to witness the performance, and obtain copies of the drama, was manifested by Mosby and the men. Private expeditions to Alexandria were proposed, but obstacles beyond our control prevented the execution of them. One day, at Joe Blackwell's, Mosby, in the presence of Stringfellow and others, expressed a desire to have a copy of the play, and also a determination to go to Alexandria and see it played. Stringfellow waited until Mosby was through; then jumping up suddenly, he mounted his horse, and without telling any one his intentions, started off alone for Alexandria. Riding rapidly, he entered the city before day the next morning, and, stopping at a trusty friend's, spent the remainder of the day in "sight-seeing" and conversing with the soldiers. Going to a book-store, he procured several copies of the play, and awaited patiently the approach of night to see it played. The play had a great run. The house was crowded, and he found difficulty in getting a seat. At twelve o'clock that night, he was again in his saddle; and next evening, at three o'clock, was back again in Fauquier, at Mosby's headquarters, with copies of the play. The rapidity of his movements, as well as his daring conduct, completely surprised the great partisan, and ever after that expedition, Stringfellow enjoyed Mosby's fullest confidence and highest esteem.

But I am digressing too much. Mosby, on the afternoon of the 7th, reflected on Stringfellow's proposition, and thinking it practicable, ordered a meeting of the whole command at Upperville the next day at twelve o'clock. The men were reluctant to leave their comfortable log fires. The mercury ranged at zero, at breakfast that morning; and the snow was one foot deep on the ground, with a fair prospect of another fall of snow during the day. Only one hundred men reported for duty. At three o'clock in the afternoon, orders were given for us to mount and fall into line of march. We moved off from Upperville, taking the road to Union, and reached Woodgrove, in Loudon County, at eight o'clock P.M., where Mosby was joined by Stringfellow with nine men, making in all, including officers, one hundred and ten effective men. After resting there some two hours, for the purpose of thoroughly warming ourselves, as well as to avoid being seen by the Union citizens in that part of the county, at ten o'clock we resumed our march, taking the high road direct to Harper's Ferry, alternately riding and walking, to keep our feet and hands, as well as bodies, warm. While riding, we would put the reins in our mouths, and our hands under the saddle-blankets, next to the horses' skins, to keep from being frozen. This road we followed until within three or four miles of the enemy's pickets, which were posted about one quarter of a mile from camp, at a small bridge over a mountain stream. Leaving the highway to our left, we took a by-path which led us into the mountains, and followed that in single file until we reached the Potomac River, across which could be distinctly seen the infantry camp-fires, and the sentry on his beat. Turning short to the left, we passed through a dense pine thicket, about two hundred yards, when we reached the bridge across the Shenandoah River. On the left of the road, at the top of a steep hill, and some twenty yards from the bridge, stood a two-story frame building, in which were the quarters of Colonel Cole and other officers. Farther up the road, about twenty yards on the right, under the mountain, were quietly reposing the objects of our pursuit. To reach this camp, as we emerged from the thicket, we had to ascend a steep hill about twenty feet high, on which the snow had been trodden until it was as hard and slick as ice. The ascent of this hill was very dangerous, and was made in single file. Yet we ascended it without accident, and were in the camp. We could touch the tents with our pistols. Mosby, with one hundred and ten men, stood there in almost the very centre of the strongest fortified post of the North on that line of defences. I could scarcely realize it. Everything so far seemed to promise success to the enterprise, and render it the most brilliant affair of the war. Not a cloud could be seen. The moon seemed to shine with her silvery light brighter than ever before. The air was still and piercing cold; not even the trampling of the horses' feet could be heard. Mosby was the first to enter the camp. He was followed by Stringfellow and his men, whom he had dispatched to the house to secure Cole and the other officers before he would take the camp, which was to be done without firing a shot. While Stringfellow was proceeding to execute his part, Mosby ordered Smith to ride back and hurry up the men, as it was of the highest importance he should make all prisoners before any alarm could be given. Montjoy was sent down the road, about one quarter of a mile, with six men, to secure the picket. He and Smith, with the rest of the men, were to enter the tents, and make prisoners of every one in them.

But, alas! by some almost unaccountable means the plan failed in an instant, from one or the other of the following causes: in front of this house where the officers were sleeping, there was a stable which was supposed to contain the officers' horses, and around were several army wagons with mules tied to them. Some few of the men left the ranks to secure the mules; and it was supposed by many of us that they spoke rather loud, and that the officers were aroused, and a shot was fired from the house; or by Stringfellow's men leaving him after he got into the house, and crossing the road, ascending the mountain and charging into the camp in the rear, yelling and firing. At the first shot from them, Mosby, thinking they were the enemy (for he had ordered that no men should enter the camp, and particularly in that manner, from that quarter), ordered the charge. Not more than thirty of us rode up to the tents, which we completely riddled by the bullets from our pistols. The enemy soon cried out, "*The camp is yours! We surrender! Stop firing!*" The firing ceased.

Stringfellow's men charging into us, produced some confusion in our ranks, and most of the men would not come into the camp, notwithstanding Mosby's orders to "*come in and secure the horses.*" The firing alarmed the picket at the bridge before Montjoy could reach them, and they fled to the mountains. The Yankees coming out of their tents, and seeing so few to surrender to, retreated to some bushes a short distance up the mountain, in the rear of their camp, and poured a most murderous fire into our little squad. Some fifty of our men were out in the road with sixty horses when the enemy rallied, and they would not come back. The position to which the enemy retreated being so strong, and our boys having fired all the loads out of their pistols, Mosby determined to retire. Our situation at this moment was indeed critical. The signal-gun at the Ferry had been fired, and the whole garrison was under arms, and ready to march at a moment's notice. Lieutenant Thomas Turner, commanding Company A, had fallen at the first fire, mortally wounded, and was carried off the field. Captain Robinson, a Scotchman, and captain in the English army, had been killed by our own men through mistake. Lieutenant Colston, of General Trimble's staff, had fallen while trying to rally the men. Two other brave spirits had likewise given up their lives in defence of Southern independence; and the gallant Charlie Paxon was lying at the entrance of a tent, mortally wounded.

Fearing reënforcements would arrive for the enemy before we could get out, Captain Smith, the last man to leave, was passing the tent where Paxon was lying, was recognized, and asked "for God's sake not to leave him." The appeal to the generous Smith could not be resisted. Suddenly whirling his horse around, and reaching down to place the dying youth in front of him, to bring him off, a Yankee in the tent shot him through the heart, and he fell lifeless to the earth, saying not a word. The heroic William Chapman came to his assistance in a moment; but the life of him whom the enemy dreaded equally as much as Mosby had fled. The enemy were advancing at the double quick, and Chapman was compelled to fly and rejoin the command. Although day was near dawning, and the whole garrison alive, the retreat was conducted in the most orderly manner, — not out of a slow walk. And, had we been pursued beyond the camp, I believe every man would have stood up like a *Stonewall* against the enemy, and revenged the death of the noble and brave spirits who had fallen that morning. The attack was at five o'clock, and in the fall of Smith and Turner, Mosby lost his ablest and most promising officers. The terror of Smith to the enemy, and the boldness of his forays, were not second to Mosby's; and Mosby's appreciation of his services as an auxiliary and an officer, and the grief he felt when told of his death, could not be better evidenced than by his crying like a child, and declining to do anything for a month. The sorrow he manifested at the loss of such a man was shared by the men and other officers.

William R. Smith was no ordinary man. Himself and his brothers before him, who had given up their lives in the cause of Southern independence, had repeatedly received compliments from Generals Lee, Ewell, and Stuart, for their bravery and daring deeds. William R. Smith was a lieutenant in the famous Black Horse Cavalry; and, when Mosby was detailed from the regular army to do this service, he requested General Stuart to let him take Smith with him. Smith was a son of Blackwell Smith, farmer, and one of the oldest, most respectable, and influential citizens in Fauquier County. He was brave and generous to a fault; his men idolized him; his conversation was of that frank and generous nature which captivated every one who met him.

Lieutenant Thomas Turner was a native of Prince George County, Maryland, and a resident of Washington City at the breaking out of the Rebellion. He was among the first from that noble old State to volunteer in the Southern cause, and was a first lieutenant in the First Regiment of Virginia Cavalry, of which Mosby was Adjutant. He was brave and courageous, and was known amongst the men as "Fighting Tom." Those qualities so essential for a partisan ranger, combined with coolness, recommended him to Mosby, who had him likewise transferred, and made him his first lieutenant. Being unable to remain on the field, Gragan and Whaley carried him to a Mr. Waters' house, about one mile from Harper's Ferry, where he lingered five days, receiving every attention our Southern friends in the neighborhood were permitted to show him. He was buried in the cemetery at Hillsboro', a beautiful little village, some ten miles from Harper's Ferry. As soon as day broke, Mosby sent back a flag of truce, under William H. Chapman and R. P. Montjoy, to get Smith's body. Reaching the pickets, and making known their mission, Colonel Cole declined to give them the body; but told Chapman any "citizen or member of his family could get it." A day or two after this, Captain Smith's wife, father, and mother went after it. On their arrival at Colonel Cole's headquarters, an order was received from General Mulligan, the commander of the post, to arrest them; and they remained under arrest forty-eight hours. General Mulligan declined to see them, or even hold any communication with them. Finally an interview was obtained with one of the adjutants of the post; and, before he would consent to give her her husband's body, Mrs. Smith was compelled to go down on her knees.

The enemy, in the meanwhile, had robbed Captain Smith of his money, watch, papers, &c.; and had absolutely taken every vestige of clothing from his body, except his drawers. Colston, Robinson, Paxon, and the two others were served in the same way, and all of them buried in a sink; and before Mrs. Smith could see the body of her husband, it had to be carried to the river and washed. Not only did the commandant of the post arrest Mrs. Smith's father and mother; but he threatened to place under arrest Colonel Cole and all his officers, for not sending Captain Chapman and Montjoy, under arrest, to his headquarters. General Mulligan, however, never carried his threat into execution. We brought off the field *sixty* fine horses, which the enemy had just drawn from the Quartermaster, and *six* prisoners, and had it not been for the loss of the brave officers and men, it would have been the most daring and brilliant affair of the war. It was a great success, anyhow: yet Colonel Cole telegraphs to Washington, "*He was attacked that morning, before daylight, by General Mosby, Colonel White, and part of Rosser's Brigade; and, after an hour's desperate fighting, the enemy were driven back, and routed with heavy loss in killed, wounded, and prisoners.*" The fight did not last fifteen minutes. We lost only one prisoner, Lem Brown; and he was taken the next morning bringing out two horses and one prisoner.

The loss of Smith, Turner, Paxon, Colston, and the others, was a severe blow to Mosby, and cast a gloom over the whole county, when it was known. The spirits of the men were in a measure broken; and although Smith and Turner were succeeded by able and brave officers, yet it was a long time before they enjoyed the same esteem and confidence that were given to Smith and Turner. Charlie Paxon was one of the most promising young men in the battalion, and, had he lived, would have distinguished himself.

CHAPTER XVII.

DESPONDENCY OF MOSBY AND HIS MEN AFTER THE HARPER'S FERRY DISASTER — CAPTURE OF A SUTLER'S WAGON, AND A CORRESPONDENT OF THE "NEW YORK TRIBUNE" — CAPTURE OF A PICKET BY MONTJOY — ORDER OF GENERAL PLEASANTON.

MOSBY had been in the habit, before this Harper's Ferry disaster, of attacking the enemy's camps in the night-time; but, ever after this, he could not be induced to entertain such a proposition, except under peculiar circumstances. This resolution was not arrived at so much from fear of the enemy's inflicting injury on him, as from the danger of his own men's firing into one another. In this case it was conceded, by all the men, that three out of the five killed were killed by our own men. So great was the despondency of the men, at the result of this affair, that nothing was done for some time. Their attachment for Smith and Turner was so great that their loss rendered the men unfit for duty. Mosby himself did not take the saddle again until February. Smith was his right-hand man; and so great was Mosby's confidence in him, that he would allow Smith to take on a raid any part or all of the command when he felt so inclined. Socially, Smith was as genial as a May day; a strict disciplinarian, who would allow none of his men to shirk duty.

In the latter part of January, 1864, R. P. Montjoy took fifteen men on an expedition to capture the United States mail, between Warrenton and the Junction on the Orange and Alexandria Railroad, the mail guarded by only twenty cavalry. It was a bold undertaking, and no man was better qualified to undertake it than Montjoy. All his men wore the regular blue army overcoats to deceive the enemy. Montjoy reached the point at which he was to make the attack, about midway between the two places, one hour too late, the mail and escort having passed by. Concealing his men in the woods, and throwing out along the road pickets to see if anything would turn up, he remained in that position a short time, when a sutler-wagon and correspondent of the "New York

Tribune" came *joggling* along. They were gobbled up in a little while. The wagon was loaded with stationery and notions. Our men, after taking what they wanted, left the wagon with the remainder of its contents in the road. The sutler parted with greenbacks &c. very reluctantly; while the correspondent took it very coolly, one of the men exchanging a Confederate hat (little worn) and homespun woollen gloves for his elegant fur cap and mink-skin gloves. As he was just from New York, he was pretty flush with greenbacks, which he was *advised* to exchange for Confederate notes, as he was going to Richmond, and these notes were the only currency permitted by law in that city, a heavy penalty being attached to the passing of greenbacks. This arrangement he readily agreed to; and he and his companion, the sutler, were started back to Fauquier under guard of one man.

Leaving that point, it being considered not safe to remain there any longer, Montjoy proceeded in the direction of a large cavalry camp. When near it he saw a sergeant posting a picket of ten men, some three hundred yards from the camp. He at once concluded to take it. The picket was in full view of the camp. Montjoy with his men approached the post, and was ordered to halt. "What command do you belong to?" cried the picket. "The First Maine Cavalry," responded Montjoy. "All right," replied the unsuspecting Yankee. The party rode up to the post, dividing and passing on either side, thus surrounding them. After some few inquiries by Montjoy, at a signal, every one of the picket had a pistol at his head, with orders to get on his horse and follow, which they did without hesitation. The sergeant highly complimented Montjoy for his daring and adroitness. The affair having been observed in camp, Montjoy was obliged to retreat precipitately with four hundred Federal cavalry after him. He, however, escaped with all his capture except the sergeant and two privates. The horses captured were retained in Fauquier County; and the prisoners, ten in number, were sent to Richmond, where accommodations were provided at *Hotel de Libby*.

The boldness and audacity of Montjoy in this affair provoked the enemy beyond bounds, and the only satisfaction they could find was the promulgation of that famous order of

General Pleasanton, wherein he ordered, " that in consequence of so many pickets, patrols, &c., being captured by parties dressed in the Federal uniform, his pickets were hereby ordered to shoot or hang every Rebel soldier caught dressed thus." This was a very sensible order,— catching before hanging. It was not the first order of the kind ever issued by the Federal Generals. And General Pleasanton knew, at the time he issued it, that his men would not, and in fact were afraid to execute it; for they knew full well there was such a law as *retaliation*, and that Mosby was the man to apply it without consulting the authorities at Richmond. Besides, they knew it would be rather an expensive *luxury* with them, as where they caught one of our men, we caught twenty of theirs; and, if they hung one of ours, twenty of theirs would pay the penalty for it. The order, however, had the effect of inducing a large number of the men to dye their overcoats black.

CHAPTER XVIII.

JOHN CORNWALL'S REVENGE—TWENTY-FIVE OF OUR MEN CAPTURED—CAPTAIN CHAPMAN'S ATTEMPT TO RESCUE THEM—THE ENEMY TAKE HORSES, CHICKENS, ETC.—MOSBY'S MEN SLEEP IN CAVES, ETC.

FEBRUARY arrived. Mosby made a flying visit to his family, which was staying then at Charlottesville, and also to Richmond. On the night of the 5th he entered Warrenton alone, and obtained valuable information respecting the enemy's strength and plans for the next campaign, which he took to Richmond, and laid before the Secretary of War. Mosby returned to his headquarters next morning; and on the 6th of the month, with John Munson and Ben Palmer, started for our lines.

During Mosby's absence, the men were not idle, but continued to annoy the enemy. The winter had broken, and the weather was never better adapted for carrying on such enterprises. Captain William H. Chapman, of Company C, assumed command of the battalion during Mosby's absence. He took twenty into the Valley of Virginia, crossing the Shenandoah River at Berry Ferry, and captured a patrolling party of thirty cavalry, near the White Post, and returned with thirty prisoners and horses, without loss or injury.

The 18th of this month will be remembered by the people of Fauquier, or rather of "Mosby's Confederacy," for all time. A trifling white man, by the name of John Cornwall, had been dodging, for twelve months, the enrolling officers, to keep out of the service, and had been employed by Captain Walter Frankland, our quartermaster, to make one trip to Charlottesville, with an ambulance, to bring back a load of ammunition. On his return, he presented a bill of expenses, a portion of which Frankland disallowed. Cornwall appealed to Mosby, who sustained Frankland. Leaving headquarters, he swore vengeance against Mosby, Frankland, and the whole command. On the 17th he went to the enemy at Warrenton, and had no difficulty in entering their lines;

for it was established as a fact, after he left, that he had been going backwards and forwards for some time, carrying information to the enemy, and stealing all the fine horses in the neighborhood, and selling them to the enemy. Going to headquarters, he stated his grievances, and offered to capture Mosby and his whole command if they would give him five hundred men. The enemy, considering his plans practicable, complied with his request; and the night of the 18th was selected for the purpose. The residents of Fauquier, and the enemy themselves who participated in that affair, will remember it as the coldest night of that severe winter. The column started from Warrenton on the 17th, at nine o'clock P.M., and reached Salem at one o'clock A.M. At this place they commenced, and searched every house up to the Blue Ridge Mountains, along and under them to Middleburg, embracing an area of about fifteen square miles. At Rectortown they divided, one half — two hundred and fifty — going by Middleburg and Upperville, where both reunited at sunrise; the other column taking in its march, Piedmont, Oak Hill, Markham, and Paris, at the foot of Ashby's Gap, thence to

Upperville. One squad of fifty even penetrated the mountains, and visited Slice Barbour's, on the top of one of the spurs of the Blue Ridge, where Cornwall behaved most disgracefully. Learning that Mosby was absent, the enemy thought they had a sure thing of it, and that, on the return of the great partisan, he would find himself minus his command; and their scheme came very near proving successful. But the Fates were against them, and a beneficent Providence had decreed otherwise.

Two things conspired in our favor, — the darkness of the night and the cold. Although their visit was unexpected, and a perfect surprise, as we had not thrown out pickets, they did not capture more than twenty-five of our men. You see we boarded and slept at the farmers' houses; and the enemy thought all they had to do was to ride up, surround the houses, go in, and take us out of bed. But the weather being so bitter cold, and they nearly frozen, the enemy could not act with much celerity. At the house of Mr. Jamison Ashby, uncle of the lamented Turner Ashby, where Captain Frankland lodged, one hundred and fifty surrounded the house, and Cornwall himself superintended the search. He said he was bound to have Frankland. The room was entered; but the bed was empty, yet warm. The cage had been opened, and the bird had flown, but not out of the house. The building was searched thoroughly three times; but Frankland could not be found. The little negroes were questioned, and threatened with instant death if they did not tell where Frankland, Henry Ashby, and Hamner were. All they could get out of the servants and little darkeys was, they did not know anything about them. The party never executed their threats, but went off disappointed, saying they would come back; but they did not do so that morning. While one set were searching the house, there was another in the stables and fields, getting the horses and mules of Mr. Ashby and his boarders. Not content with all the horses on the place, they stole every turkey, chicken, duck, and goose on the plantation. I will here state, for the information of my readers, that Captain Frankland could see and hear all that was going on in the house. When the enemy approached Ben Triplett's, where Lieutenant

Albert Wren and Jim Wren boarded, the men jumped out of the second-story window in their night-clothes, and fled across the fields, pursued by the enemy, and sought refuge in a straw-rick, under the mountain, on the opposite side of " Crooked Run." The enemy ceased their pursuit at the Run. In this rick the two remained for three hours, and at daylight were found nearly frozen; but, by proper remedies, they were soon restored, and enabled to participate with the heroic Chapman in his efforts to recapture our boys that day. Others made equally narrow escapes, and suffered from the cold as severely.

At Mr. Gibson's, Sergeant Corbin, when the enemy declared that if he, Walston, and the three Gibsons did not come out and give themselves up, the house would be burnt, came out and surrendered, to save the others. While all this was going on, the brave William H. Chapman was collecting together what men he could. He succeeded in getting thirty, and attacked the enemy about one mile from Paris, on Mrs. Betsy Edmond's farm. The enemy retreated to a field in front of her house, and drew up in line of battle behind a stone fence. Not wishing to sacrifice his men by attacking them in that position, Chapman retired a short distance to watch their movements. In a short time the enemy received reënforcements from Paris, when they all retreated to that place, and remained until three o'clock P.M., when they started back to Warrenton. About noon Mosby returned from Richmond; and, hearing of the calamity Cornwall had brought upon him, determined, if possible, to rescue his men, and capture Cornwall. Collecting every man he possibly could, he tried to divide the enemy so as to attack him in detail; which, if he had succeeded in doing, he would have not only got his own men back, but a large number of the enemy. The enemy, however, kept well closed up on their return; and there was no possible chance of cutting any of them off. Then, as a last resort for the recapture of his men, he determined to attack the enemy near Warrenton. Taking a private road, he expected to reach the point at which he intended to make the attack some time before the enemy, and to stretch a large piece of telegraph wire across the road, and, when they approached it, to charge them in the rear, and run them against it in the dark. But they, apprehending some trick would be played upon them by us in the dark, marched in a trot, and reached Warrenton at sunset, with all their prisoners, turkeys, chickens, &c. They took back with them two hundred of the finest horses in the State of Virginia. The citizens of Warrenton told us that this raiding party, on their return, had turkey and roast chicken for dinner one whole week afterwards.

After this night raid to " Mosby's Confederacy," the boys built huts in the mountains, but would take their meals as heretofore, and after supper, or at dark, would repair with their horses to the huts, and repose as comfortably as in feather-beds. Some slept in caves in the mountains; some continued to remain as before, but had burrowed holes in the ground under the houses, which were entered through a trap-door. When the " British " (Sam Alexander's name of the enemy) came, they could seek refuge in the holes; the houses being hid in the woods. Others had niches, with small holes for the eyes made in the walls of the houses; these niches being entered by private doors. Some few would secrete themselves up the chimneys. Mosby, with one or two of his *staff*, and often by himself, would generally, at dark, mount their horses, and go down to some good friend's house near the enemy's camps, and stay all night, thinking that the safest place.

CHAPTER XIX.

AFFAIR AT DRANESVILLE—ATTACK UPON COLONEL COLE—"PRIVATE" OPERATIONS—MOSBY LIES IN WAIT FOR A DETATCHMENT—EVACUATION OF WARRENTON—RAID INTO THE VALLEY.

THE success of this last raid produced the greatest rejoicing throughout the North. The enemy were sure they had crippled Mosby beyond his ability to recuperate. The officers commanding the expedition were lauded to the skies. The California battalion, stationed at Vienna, concluded to finish him entirely, and terminate his career as a partisan. Accordingly, a raid was made by two hundred and fifty men, who, after scouring the upper portion of Fauquier, without seeing him, his men, or anything else, returned in the hope that he had left the country, as he could no longer hold it. Mosby, hearing them coming, collected eighty of his men, and started for Dranesville, a little village in

Prince William County. Knowing the enemy would pass through the place on their return to camp, Mosby placed twenty-five of his men in ambush, on each side of the road, just outside of the town, and divided the rest, so that one half should attack in front, while the other half charged them in the rear, thus subjecting them to a fire all around. In the course of an hour, the enemy approached in a very careless manner. The men in ambush opened on them with Colt's army-pistols, producing confusion in their ranks. Before order was restored, they were attacked in the rear and front; Mosby leading the latter. Desperate was the fighting, and terrible the slaughter; a large portion of the fighting being hand to hand. Numbers fought their way through our thin ranks, and escaped. Fifty of the enemy were killed and wounded and left on the field; seventy prisoners and ninety horses were brought off the field. The most remarkable feature about the affair was, that Mosby lost only *one* man killed (Chapplier of Fauquier,) and three wounded.

In the month of March, Colonel Cole made his farewell raid into our "Confederacy."

Mosby was at Piedmont, receiving the congratulations of some of his men on his promotion to the rank of Lieutenant-Colonel. Cole dashed in on the party, and dispersed them, capturing two or three. Mosby, rallying his men, and by the coming in of others having his force increased to seventy-five effective men, followed up Cole, whose force numbered two hundred and fifty, and attacked him at the schoolhouse, three miles from Upperville, on the road to Bloomfield, and routed them, driving them ten miles, killing and wounding twenty. One killed they left in the road, and he was buried in the lot adjoining the schoolhouse; Mosby sustaining no loss. Twenty horses were secured in this little affair. The rest of this month no raids took place; but numerous *private* scouting-parties operated on the enemy, obtaining valuable information, and doing good service. The brave and lamented Watt Bowie, of Maryland, Bush and Sam Underwood, John W. Puryear, of Richmond, John Russell, of Clark County, Virginia, and others commanded these parties. Bowie operated in Maryland, the Underwoods in Fairfax, Russell, Puryear, and others operated in the valley. They would return, some mornings, loaded with plunder, prisoners, and horses, captured from the enemy.

Early in April, Colonel Mosby received *information*, from a reliable source, that the enemy at Warrenton contemplated another raid into his Confederacy. There was general rejoicing throughout the command at their expected visit. Mosby, acting on this information, ordered every man to repair to Somerset Mills, on the road from Piedmont to Ashby's Gap. Two hundred men reported for duty. At dark we moved from Somerset to the woods adjoining Mrs. Shacklett's farm, one mile from Piedmont, and lay there three consecutive nights, awaiting the approach of the enemy; but the enemy did not come; and most fortunate was it for them that they did not, for very few would have got back to camp to tell the tale. Each of our men was armed with a double-barrelled shot-gun (each barrel with twenty-four buckshot in it), besides three brace of Colt's pistols, which were good for twelve more shots. What execution these would have done, I leave for my readers to determine.

General Grant, having assumed command

of the Army of the Potomac about this time, commenced his advance "on to Richmond," expecting to walk rough-shod over General Lee, and celebrate his Fourth of July in that city. Warrenton was evacuated, much to the relief of its citizens. At this place they left articles which betrayed the traps they had set for us, which consisted of wires stretched across the streets, to sweep us off our horses if we dashed into the place during their occupation of it; but we had warm friends there, who kept us always posted in regard to the intentions of the enemy and what they were doing. Nothing could transpire in Warrenton during the day, which we would not know at headquarters before twelve o'clock the same night.

A few days after the evacuation of Warrenton, Chapman and Montjoy carried fifty of us down to the place to capture a scouting-party of the enemy, numbering seventy-five or a hundred. We arrived in town too late, the enemy having gone about one hour before. Our entrance into Warrenton was very gratifying to the men. Smiles and waving of white handkerchiefs, from fair young ladies, greeted us from every house; and there was a general rejoicing. Cakes, wine, &c. (just think of it, kind reader), were handed around by pretty ladies to a set of guerillas, who had nothing to drink in their Confederacy but new wheat whiskey and apple brandy just from the still. As we entered the town, desolation met the eye from every quarter. Warrenton, which, in time of peace, abounded in beautiful groves, flowers, and green fields, was now like a deserted ship at sea. The beautiful groves had been cut down to afford fuel to the soldiers; fences gone; private grounds and buildings converted into stables; and, in the place of the luxuriant fields, ugly mud huts could be seen as far as the eye could reach. Everything inviting and pleasant to the sight had disappeared, except the pretty girls and the houses they lived in. Remaining in town not more than an hour, we returned to headquarters to prepare for a raid into the valley the next day. Agreeably to orders, we met at Paris the next day. · Colonel Mosby made a detail of twenty-five men, and started for the valley. Crossing the Blue Ridge at Ashby's Gap, and swimming the Shenandoah River at Berry's Ferry, near Winchester, he captured a small wagon-train and ten horses and six prisoners, and sent them out to Fauquier, by Cuper and three others. Pushing on with the rest of his men (twenty), he reached Martinsburg a little after midnight. After a little reconoitring he dismounted part of his men (the rest holding their horses), and entered the enemy's camp about one mile from town. The officers being absent on a frolic in the town, the guards were careless. Our men entered the stables, and brought out twenty fine horses. The guards were aroused; and our men, upon leaving the stables, were fired upon, but no one on our side was injured. Some of the men entered the officers' tents, and secured their entire wardrobes. Mosby and Wirt Ashby entered the town, and inspected the enemy's fortifications, rejoining the men without discovery. The Yankee officers, on their return to quarters, did not miss anything until ten o'clock the next morning, when, to their astonishment, they discovered that twenty of their finest horses were gone. By the time the discovery was made, Mosby was across the Shenandoah River, in Paris, distributing the prizes amongst his men. There were horses in this lot which Louis Napoleon would have been proud to own; yet Mosby would not appropriate a single one to his own use. During his whole career as a partisan, of the many thousand horses — and very fine ones too — which he captured, he appropriated but one captured horse to his own use. This he did when General Lee invaded Pennsylvania, in 1863. General Stuart was passing through Upperville upon a very indifferent horse. Mosby, feeling a little mortified at the condition of the General's horse, dismounted from a very fine mare, and presented it to the General. Mosby then mounted Stuart's horse, and, crossing the mountains into the valley, captured a vidette that night, and returned to Fauquier before day the next morning.

CHAPTER XX.

EXPLOIT OF LIEUTENANT CHAPMAN — VISIT OF A GERMAN BARON — "GOING THROUGH" — OUR "TACTICS" — NARROW ESCAPE — CAPTURES OF WAGONS, ETC.

LIEUTENANT SAMUEL CHAPMAN, brother of Captain William H. Chapman, who had distinguished himself on several battle-fields by his bravery, was this month transferred to the battalion from the regular army, at the special request of Colonel Mosby, who appointed him his Adjutant, with the rank of First Lieutenant. Lieutenant Chapman, a few days after his arrival in Fauquier, took fifty men, crossed the mountains at Slice Barbour's, and the Shenandoah River at Howardsville, and attacked, in the night-time, a picket-post of one hundred of the enemy at Guard Hill, and captured thirty prisoners, including one captain, and fifty horses, besides killing and wounding several, and returned without loss.

Mosby's fame as a successful partisan ranger, was at its zenith, and had reached the Old World. Officers in the European armies came over, and joined him as privates. One German baron came out from Washington to see Mosby, and learn his *tactics* and the great secret of his success. On his way up to our headquarters, from Washington City, he met with some of our scouts in Fairfax County. He told them his business: but they took him to be an impostor and spy; and, acting upon that supposition, they "*went through* him." As I have used this phrase very often, I deem it proper my readers should know what it means, and the *modus operandi*. Meeting an enemy after his surrender, you demand his greenbacks. If he is slow in shelling out, you simply insert your hand into his pocket and take them, or present a pistol to his head. The latter was the most popular method; and, finally, it got to be a common course on both sides, that the captured, after his arms were taken away, always handed the captor his pocket-book without being asked. If he had a watch, he was relieved of that, lest it might be taken from him on his way to Richmond. If his hat was better than yours, you exchanged with him, and the same way with boots and everything else. My readers will please to understand we were not the only ones who indulged in this luxury. Our enemies indulged in it in every instance, and particularly the officers, even those as high in rank as colonel.

But to return to our baron. He remonstrated with his captors all in vain. After relieving him of his valuables, they let him pass on; and he reached Mosby's headquarters. He reported his treatment, and asked redress. After an examination of his papers and his business, he was politely informed that that "was part of our tactics." The baron returned to Washington a poorer but wiser man.

During this month, details were made to go to Loudon County, to collect forage for the ensuing campaign, which promised to be a very active one. Grant had fought the battle of Spottsylvania Court House, and was repulsed. General Lee, fearing his supplies would be cut off, reoccupied his old lines at

Fredericksburg, and gave his adversary a severe drubbing there. Citizens of that ancient town were turned out of their homes to accommodate the enemy's wounded, which numbered thirty thousand.

Just after the battle of Fredericksburg, Mosby took fifty men, well-mounted, to King George's County, below Fredericksburg, and captured a wagon-train, and brought out forty mules and horses and ten prisoners, without loss. He was absent five days. Having been so successful on the last raid, Mosby ordered fifty more of us to meet him at Joe Blackwell's, the day after his return, with *five* days' feed for our horses. Rations for ourselves we never carried, depending on buying or having them given to us by the citizens. We moved from headquarters at noon, and bivouacked the first night out near Catlett's Station, on the Orange and Alexandria Railroad. At daylight the next morning we crossed the railroad, and took the old telegraph road to within a mile of Stafford Court House. Leaving the highway about half a mile, we entered one of those deep ravines which abound in that rugged country, and remained until the next afternoon, when we

GEORGE BAYLOR.

resumed our march, passing through Stafford Court House, thence across the Acquia Creek Railroad, to a secluded point about three miles from Belle Plains. Here we were rejoined by Mosby, Charlie Hall, and John Edmonds, who had been on a scouting-party to find out the wagon-trains from the Plains to Fredericksburg. While out, they captured a wagon-master, who had strayed away from his train, from whom they obtained all the information necessary for Mosby to carry out his plans. While they were interrogating him, a brigade of infantry was seen approaching them. Mosby sent his prisoner into the woods, out of their view, while he and Edmonds remained in the road. As the brigade passed, Mosby and Edmonds exchanged salutes, and conversed with the officers " on the situation." After the column had passed, Mosby and his party returned to the command, reaching it early in the afternoon. At midnight we started out to find the wagon-camp. On the march we had a fine view, by moonlight, of the enemy's fleet at the mouth of Acquia Creek. It had the appearance of a large city lighted by gas. A diligent search was instituted for the camp, but it was not found until near daylight. It was not guarded; but, daylight being so near, Mosby deferred the attack until next night, with the view of making a sure thing of it. Had the nights that season of the year been one or two hours longer, Mosby would have made a capture which would have eclipsed all his former deeds.

From Belle Plains to Fredericksburg the distance is nine miles, and the enemy had a train of wagons hauling supplies from this place to the latter for the army. Indeed, so numerous were the enemy, that, to facilitate this immense amount of transportation, two roads were required, one for the wagons to go up, and the other to return. The remoteness of this country from our headquarters, Fauquier, induced the enemy to believe we would not molest them; consequently, they dispensed with the usual guards. Besides, Grant had lost so heavily at Spottsylvania and Fredericksburg, that every soldier was needed in the field. When it was known the camp was found, the men were anxious to "go into it" anyhow. The temptation was great, but had to be resisted; for had we attacked it, and captured five hundred or a thousand mules and horses, we could have at that hour been cut off and captured. Mosby took us back to the dense pine woods, to await the return of night. At ten o'clock Mosby left us in charge of Alfred Glasscock, who was to make the attack, and went scouting to Fairfax County.

The enemy, in small squads, started out the next morning, to see if any rebels were in that country. Seeing the tracks we made the night before, they returned to camp, and reported. Then a force of one regiment of cavalry and one regiment of infantry were started out to capture us. While most of us were indulging ourselves in a nap, under the shade of the trees, some with their horses unsaddled, our men were suddenly confronted with a large column of infantry. They, not knowing our force, halted, which afforded our pickets time to get back to camp, and apprise us of our danger. In a few moments we were mounted, and ready to move; but our guide, Charlie Hall, was gone. We, however, commenced the retreat, going in the direction of the railroad. Meeting a citizen hiding from the enemy, we were advised by him not to "go that way;" that "the whole country was filled with the enemy." There being no one amongst us who knew the country, he guided us to the railroad, where we met another detachment of infantry marching down the railroad with laborers to repair it. Being thus cut off, Glasscock adopted the daring plan of dashing on (we after him), and crying out, "Mosby is after us! get out of the way!" The enemy broke, and ran for the woods; we passed, and got out safe.

That morning, early, Charlie Hall (our guide) and John Edmonds had started out scouting; and, as they had not returned before we left, the greatest anxiety was felt for their safety. They came out safe, with three prisoners and horses, but with some difficulty. On their return to camp, they met this same force, and were compelled to change their course. Whatever way they went, the enemy's pickets were seen. Finding themselves surrounded, to save their prisoners and horses, they concluded to represent themselves as a federal scouting-party looking for Mosby. Riding up to the pickets, and representing themselves as such, they were permitted to pass out of their lines, and got back safe to Fauquier with their booty.

CHAPTER XXI.

CAPTURE OF A VIDETTE BY JOHN RUSSELL—DISAPPOINTMENTS—VARIOUS OPERATIONS—BOB WALKER, LIKE CHARLES SECOND, ESCAPES BY CLIMBING A TREE—KEYES'S CAVALRY.

IN a few days after our return, Mosby (not seeing anything in Fairfax for us) took one hundred and fifty men to the valley, crossing the mountains at Ashby's Gap, and swimming the Shenandoah River at Berry's Ferry, pushed on under cover of night to Martinsburg, to capture one hundred cavalry and two hundred artillery horses. We reached the suburbs of the town about three o'clock A.M., without being seen by any one, and halted under a hill near the railroad, while Mosby and John Russell should reconnoitre, and find out the best way to get in. To their surprise, three hundred infantry were found guarding the horses, and videttes were found posted a hundred yards apart all around the camp. Mosby at once abandoned all idea of attacking the camp, and ordered us to retire. On going out we had not proceeded more than one hundred yards before the command, "Halt! who comes dar?" rang in our ears. John Russell, our guide, being in the advance, rode up to him. He was a German, and asked Russell, "Vot you want?" his carbine pointing at Russell's breast. Russell pushed his carbine aside, and, pointing a pistol in his face ordered him to throw the carbine down.

"Vot you want me throw it way for? Me pay for it."

After the exchange of a few more words, Russell, with his prisoner, joined the command, and all started back for Fauquier. At sunrise Mosby ordered A. E. Richards, who had been promoted to the captaincy of Company B, for meritorious conduct, to detail twenty men, and return to the Baltimore and Ohio Railroad, and take that express-train which passed while we were lying near Martinsburg the night before. Richards made the detail, including Lieutenant Harry Hatcher, alias "Deadly," of Company A, and returned the next night. They reached the railroad without being discovered by the pickets. There were two tracks, the old one and a new one; and they, thinking the train would pass over the new, removed a rail on it, and retired to a small piece of woods some twenty yards from the road, and then patiently awaited its arrival, each one having visions of greenbacks, gold watches, &c., &c., looming up before them. In a few moments the train came dashing by, but on the old track. One fellow, thinking it would stop for him, mounted his horse and made for it; but it soon disappeared behind a mountain, and Richards returned without accomplishing anything.

The season for a vigorous campaign approaching, Mosby, to be prepared for it, sent Companies B and C to Loudon County, to get forage for the battalion. Chapman, with Company C, collected it near Lovettsville, and pressed wagons from the farmers to send it to Fauquier. Richards, with Company B, operated in the neighborhood of Waterford, sending out with each load one or two men as a guard. Chapman gathered his without interruption. Richards, after collecting the tithe around Waterford, took his remaining men, six in number, and moved over towards Berlin to find corn for another occasion. While going down the *grade* beyond General Wright's (who was a wealthy and influential farmer at the commencement of the war, but was broken up by the enemy), we were attacked by Keyes's cavalry, sixty in number. We retreated to the woods; and, striking a private road, we followed that, which led us to the mountains, pursued all the way. Bob Walker, with Captain Richards, while gallantly trying to keep back the foe, had his horse shot under him. Being near a wheat-field, he retreated to that, climbed an apple-tree, and escaped, although the enemy instituted a diligent search for him. Reaching the mountains, we ascended them; and, resting our horses until the cool of the evening, we then resumed our march back to old Fauquier.

This affair being the first time Keyes's men ever pursued any of us, they were very much emboldened, and afterwards would cross the Potomac River at the Point of Rocks, in squads of fifteen and twenty, and scout up as far as Hamilton, Woodgrove, and Waterford, robbing the citizens who sympathized with the South, and getting whiskey at Downey's Stillhouse, the owner of which was President of the *bogus* Virginia Senate, then holding its sessions in Alexandria. This place was a great rendezvous for them, at which they captured quite a number of our men; and from this place they would come up to Waterford, a distance of only five miles, to see their parents and sweethearts. It was on one of these trips, that Lieutenant Frank Williams, of Company B, gave a drubbing to a party of them, which effectually terminated all future expeditions of the kind.

Lieutenant Williams, with six men, visited Waterford with the view of capturing one of these parties. Passing through the town, he concealed his men behind an old house near the bridge, at the lower part. In a short time fifteen of Keyes's men dashed into the village, and commenced having "a nice time" with their friends; telling them how they had chased "those horse-thieves," meaning Mosby's men, and expressing a strong desire to met them again. Williams, with one man, rode up to where they were, and fired into them. They soon mounted their horses, and gave Williams chase. When they had reached their comrades, they halted; and the rest of his men charged the enemy. Keyes retreated in confusion, and was pursued three miles. Six of his men were captured, one killed in the town, and three wounded. Williams secured ten fine horses in this little affair. When he returned to Waterford, to convey the prisoners, and look after the wounded, the most affecting scenes took place between the prisoners and their friends at parting. Williams sustained neither loss nor injury.

CHAPTER XXII.

CHARGE OF BUSHWHACKING — A DARKEY BUSHWHACKER — UNION CITIZENS OF WATERFORD — A "TRAP" — ARTILLERY — SURRENDER AT DUFFIELD — LIEUTENANT NELSON.

THE enemy, while we occupied that country, very ungenerously accused us and our Southern friends living inside their lines with being bushwhackers. Now I will venture to say here to the world, and to state it without fear of contradiction, that there were not two persons, soldiers or citizens, in that whole country, extending from the Blue Ridge to Washington, who were regular bushwhackers. The only instance of the kind that ever came to my knowledge was that of a darkey (whom the Yankees had driven away from his home) near Salem, while General Meade's army was lying around Warrenton, and scouting-parties were roving over the whole country. This darkey would take his double-barrelled shot-gun, secrete himself in the corner of the fence, amongst some bushes, and pick up the stragglers. What he did with his prisoners was never known; but I learned, from a reliable source, that he sent them to *Culpepper*. This darkey would frequently have eight and ten horses at a time. This explanation, I trust, is satisfactory, so far as regards Southern bushwhackers.

Now, a word concerning the Union citizens in and around Waterford. That place, in my judgment, afforded more of that class of people, during the war, than any other town or county in Eastern Virginia. Whenever we were in that particular portion of Loudon, our pickets were invariably fired upon by them. Information reached Mosby that the enemy had laid a trap in Loudon to capture him; and he, being a person ever ready to acquire knowledge, ordered a meeting of the command at Upperville, on the 1st of June, that they might *go up* with him. One hundred men reported for duty. Captain Richards, with Company B, he sent ahead to the neighborhood of Point of Rocks, to toll the enemy over the river, while he took Companies A and C with him. Our movements were made under cover of night, the main roads being shunned, to avoid being seen, and to keep the people ignorant of our actual strength. In the daytime we stayed in the woods, and were not allowed to expose ourselves to any one. Reaching the turnpike leading to Berlin, Mosby distributed his men in squads along this thoroughfare, in striking-distance of each other, and patiently awaited the approach of the enemy. Captain Richards being unable to draw the enemy across the river, from their stronghold at Point of Rocks, Mosby and ten men went to Harper's Ferry, to draw them out from that place. The men had not smelt gunpowder for nearly one month now, and were " spiling for a fight." Company B was ordered to Hillsboro', in hopes the enemy could be tolled from the Ferry. In such a contingency, they were to hold them in check until the rest of the men could be brought up. Company B remained here three days, and no signs of an attack. We returned to Fauquier, and to this day have never learned what that trap was which the enemy had set for us. During our stay we were most hospitably entertained by some of their citizens. Mr. Janney's and Mr.

Hoe's accomplished wives and daughters were unremitting in their attentions to us; and music, dancing, card-playing, &c., was the order for three whole days.

On the 22d of June, the battalion met at Rectortown, where we had roll-call for the first time since our organization. Two hundred and sixty men answered to their names; and, for the first time, we had one piece of artillery (twelve-pound howitzer). Detail of artillerists was made to man the gun, and Lieutenant Sam Chapman placed in command of it. At noon the men fell into ranks, and moved off in the direction of Fairfax. On reaching Anandale, we found the enemy prepared to receive us, and also reënforced. Declining to attack them, Mosby ordered us back to Fauquier by companies, Captain Richards, with Company B, taking the road, *via* Centreville and Manassas. When near Centreville he met with a large squad of the enemy, grazing their horses and surveying land (for what purpose the writer never learned). Charging them before they could form, he took thirty-five of them prisoners, killed, wounded, and dispersed the rest, secured fifty horses, and got back to Fauquier County without loss.

On the 28th day of June, a meeting was held at Upperville. Two hundred and fifty men responded to their names. At noon we moved up the turnpike through Paris; thence across the mountains at Ashby Gap. One mile from the Gap, at Mount Carmel, we took the mountain road, which carried us to Shepperd's Mills, crossing the Shenandoah River there. Resting our horses an hour or so, we resumed our march, passing through Cabletown, on to within one mile of Charlestown, on the turnpike, where we halted and drew up in line of battle on either side of the road, with one piece of artillery posted on an eminence commanding the turnpike up and down for one mile. A party was sent into town to draw the enemy out, if any were there; if not, to Halltown, near Harper's Ferry.

After waiting half an hour to be attacked, and the party sent out to draw the enemy on having returned with intelligence of no enemy nearer than Harper's Ferry, Mosby determined to strike the Baltimore and Ohio Railroad. Passing through Charlestown, where we were greeted with waving of handkerchiefs and smiles from pretty ladies, we filed off to the left, outside of the town, and made for Duffield Station, leaving Company A (twenty-five men) with Lieutenant Joseph Nelson, to prevent, if possible, our being cut off by troops from the Ferry. Reaching the railroad without opposition, Mosby sent Captain Richards into Duffield, with flag of truce, demanding an unconditional surrender, on pain of being shelled in two minutes; Mosby in the meanwhile having posted his howitzer in good position, with Company C to support it. So great was the surprise that the lieutenant of the post had to arrange the terms, the commandant being taken very suddenly sick. Richards returned with the terms, and we occupied the place. The camp was burnt, and all Government goods in the depot confiscated, including Union men's shoes, and ladies' and gentlemen's dress and fancy goods. Groceries were found in great quantities, with which each man filled his sack. The whole guard was surrendered, but only seventy infantry prisoners were brought away. Mosby, apprehending a large force might be sent from Harper's Ferry to intercept him, ordered the retreat to where Nelson was.

Mosby's expectations were realized. Before we were out of sight of Duffield, a courier came to direct us " to hurry back, as

Nelson was engaging an overwhelming force." We hurried back as fast as our horses would carry us, with the loads on them, but arrived too late for the *fun*. Nelson had already, with his twenty-five men, fought and routed one hundred of Siegel's cavalry, killing two captains, and taking twenty of them prisoners, with their horses. Nelson drove the enemy as far as Halltown. Apprehending a stronger force would be sent after us, the whole command started for Fauquier. On the way out, when above Charlestown a short distance, Siegel came down from his stronghold with a force, and displayed them one mile and a half from us, and marched back. No further attempt was made to pursue, although this dispatch was sent to Washington: "*A competent force has been sent in pursuit, and a fair prospect they will be overhauled.*" We recrossed the Shenandoah River at Shepperd's Mills that night, and camped on the Fauquier side. Next morning at daylight our march was resumed, and we reached Paris at late breakfast. Here a division of the property was made amongst the men, who were then disbanded, and the prisoners sent to Richmond.

18*

CHAPTER XXIII.

GOING INTO MARYLAND — STRICT ORDER IN MARCHING — SKIRMISHING ACROSS THE POTOMAC — A DINING PARTY INTERRUPTED — THE EAGLE CAKE — "GOING THROUGH" — YOUNG MARTIN.

THE weather being so very hot, nothing was done until the 3d day of July, when the whole command met at Upperville. The men turned out on their finest horses, each provided with a large sack strapped to his saddles, for the purpose of bringing home the plunder. The men had a presentiment that Mosby was going into Maryland, and a very correct one it was; for Generals Early and Breckenridge had commenced that celebrated movement on Washington City, and the advance was crossing the Potomac River at Williamsport. At noon the men were formed by companies, and moved off with one piece of artillery, taking the road to Bloomfield. On reaching Green Garden

Mills, one mile from Upperville, the battalion was halted, horses fed, and ammunition distributed (two rounds to a man). The sun being so intolerably hot (mercury at ninety-six in the shade), we remained here in the shade until four o'clock in the afternoon, when we formed again and moved off. All villages, Union men's houses, and public roads were avoided on the march until night. Strict orders were issued by Colonel Mosby, prohibiting the men from straggling, and telling the people to whose command they belonged. The first night out we bivouacked near Purcellville, Loudon County. At daylight, on the 4th, we resumed our march; passing through that portion of Loudon in which resided a great many people who, to curry favor with the enemy, and get pay for so doing, were continually giving information concerning our movements. It was of the highest importance, to insure success to Colonel Mosby's plans, that the citizens should be kept ignorant of the name of our command and commander; so, when any citizen inquired who we were, the men would say, "the advance guard of Longstreet's corps," knowing that it would be immediately communicated across the river, and operate to our advantage. To give plausibility to the statement, they had received intelligence that Early and Breckenridge were already in Maryland, and marching on Frederick City.

At eleven o'clock we reached the Potomac opposite Berlin, and in full view of the place; then filing right down the river through a large orchard, a few miles' march brought us to the farm of Mr. B. There we rested our horses for fully one hour, to await the return of a small scouting-party. Colonel Mosby had sent to the Point of Rocks, to look at the "situation." While waiting, and enjoying the delightful shade of the woods, a large number of the men were hospitably entertained by Mr. B.'s lady and amiable daughter, although they were strong Union people. At noon the scouting-party returned, and the order was given to "mount your horses." We then moved farther down the river, to a private ford, one mile from town, the battalion halting some two hundred yards from the river, in the woods. Sharpshooters and "long-range" guns were ordered "to the front," and skirmishing across the river commenced, Colonel Mosby superintending and participating himself in the luxury. The enemy, apprehending an attack on this stronghold, had increased the garrison at this place, and thrown up a very formidable earthwork on a knoll of ground at the lower end of the village, with a canal and river between us, in which fifty resolute men could have kept at bay, and even repulsed, at least one thousand cavalry, after the bridge across the canal was torn up. This fort commanded the river up and down for miles. The enemy's cavalry (about one hundred), commanded by Captain Keyes, 'were stationed half a mile in the rear of the town, while their infantry, some five hundred in number, were distributed on the side of the mountains for a mile up the river, and kept up a very brisk firing, without inflicting any injury to our men.

While this sharpshooting was going on, Lieutenant Sam Chapman moved his piece of artillery up a high hill directly opposite the town, and screened from the sight of the enemy, by the thick undergrowth, part of Company C supporting it. Some of the enemy were having a 4th of July dinner on a canal-boat. The dinner was over, and refreshments were being served. The sun was a little past meridian; and they seemed to be enjoying themselves so much, that it looked like a pity to break up their "sociable" in such an unceremonious manner. But the view of the enemy by the gallant and impetuous Chapman aroused that inordinate desire in him to engage them whenever and wherever he could. Placing his gun in position, he determined to fire a salute. The salute was fired, and the shell exploded under the dinner-table on the boat. A panic ensued in the town, which soon extended to the garrison. The cavalry tore up the bridge across the canal, and retreated to Frederick City, while the infantry dropped their guns, and sought refuge in the mountains, some concealing themselves in the crevices of the rocks, with the impression on their minds that the whole of Longstreet's corps was after them. Companies A, B, and D charged across the river, while the sharpshooters waded across with water up to their armpits. The scene was new to me, and the most exciting I ever experienced in my life. A few of the enemy's sharpshooters continued to fire on us while crossing, without injury to any one. The Potomac was very broad at the place we crossed, but the Maryland shore was soon reached, when our course was directed down the tow-path to the town, each man spurring on his horse, and trying to be the first in the place.

On reaching the bridge across the canal, it was found that the enemy had removed the flooring. A few minutes' time was all that was required to replace it with boards from an old warehouse on the river-banks, which the enemy occupied as quarters. In their hasty retreat from it, they forgot their colors, which we secured. A temporary floor to the bridge being laid by this time, over the boys dashed, led by Wirt Ashby, a relation of the heroic and lamented Turner Ashby. The telegraph wires were cut to prevent communication with the enemy at Harper's Ferry. On the men dashed to the enemy's camps, which, after a critical examination "for arms," were burnt. Captain Richards, with eight men, pursued the cavalry five miles beyond the town towards Frederick, but could not overtake them, when he ordered us back to the command. Passing through the burning camps, the boys, after collecting what relics they wanted, pushed on back to town. Such an exciting and laughable scene few have ever witnessed or enjoyed. They had secured a huge pound-cake, which had been prepared by some ladies, who were to give the officers of the garrison an entertainment that evening.

The history of this cake is as follows: The officers of the garrison had signified to some of their lady friends their desire and intention of celebrating the Fourth of July in a becoming manner; so their lady friends went to work and prepared a monster cake for the occasion. This cake was moulded in the form of a spread eagle, the mould being made in Boston, and measured twenty-five feet from the tip of its bill to the tip of its tail. It was a complete eagle in all its parts. It had glass eyes, talons, &c., &c., and in the baking of it, which occupied three days and nights, it was burnt (intentionally I presume), so that it looked like a real eagle. But the most remarkable thing about it was, that inside of it there was some machinery that every time one of the boys thrust his sabre into the eagle to cut off a piece, the bird would scream. What their idea was in inserting this instrument into this spread-eagle cake, I have never been able to learn or conceive. I inquired diligently of the residents of the place, but they would give us no satisfaction. Colonel Mosby would have brought it across the river, and sent it to Richmond; but the enemy had destroyed all the boats, so the boys concluded to take it to pieces; which, being done, it was with great difficulty got across the river in the evening by means of a raft. A six-horse team belonging to Mr. S. was pressed into service, the cake put into it, and started for Fauquier County. A guard of five men accompanied the wagon.

While in camp on Goose Creek, the second night they were out, the guard got drunk on "blockade," and all of them lay down and went to sleep. The driver being a strong Union man, and having conceived the idea he would be made a hero, if he could save what was left of the great American bird, availed himself of the opportunity, and drove his load in the night to a Mr. ———'s farm, in Loudon County, situated on Goose Creek. Securing four of Mr. ———'s most reliable colored servants, he secreted his precious load in one of those safe places which abound on that stream, and which are known only by those patriotic and loyal colored men, and started back with his team. Sunrise next morning, found him in the bosom of his family, on the banks of the classic Potomac. This Union driver kept the part he had played a profound secret, until General ———, occupied the valley, when he divulged his secret to him. On General ———'s retreat from Washington, a portion of his wagon-train and eight hundred prisoners crossed the Blue Ridge mountains at Ashby's Gap. This portion of his army was pursued by General Durfea, with two thousand five hundred cavalry. After occupying the Gap three days, Durfea fell back to Snickersville, where General Wright was encamped with a division of the Union army. On their march to Wright, they passed by Mr. ———'s house, and found these colored Union citizens, who conducted them to the spot where the treasure was hid, and carried it off with them. But the fates seemed opposed to having the remnants of the bird ever reaching the shores of Maryland again. Notwithstanding its long captivity, it retained signs of life still; and as it approached the soil on which the stars and stripes had never ceased to wave, those symptoms of vitality increased. An escort was sent with it; while crossing the Shenandoah River at Rock Ford, the wagon upset, and the load was precipitated into the river. By an eye-witness of the scene, I was told that it was beyond description. Suffice it to say, the greatest confusion prevailed. Every one wanted his own plan adopted to save the bird, and before any one that the men suggested could be adopted, to their utmost dismay and horror the bird gave one shriek, and then sunk to rise no more. I never learned whether or no it was recovered; the presumption is that it was not.

But I find myself digressing from my narrative. The boys enjoyed the spread-eagle cake and " blockade ". *hugely*, and many a toast was drunk, " hoping the Yankees would soon give us another thing as good as this." The contents of five stores were appropriated to themselves by the men. Some, " to make it pay," doffed their hats, and substituted a dozen Shaker bonnets, &c., &c. One fellow (Sam), the very personification of a partisan ranger, seeing the excellent "blockade" poured into the streets, thought it a wanton destruction. He conceived the idea of carrying some of it to Fauquier in his sack, which was already filled to overflowing with ladies' and gentlemen's dress and fancy goods, tea, sugar, coffee, &c. Taking this sack and putting the mouth of it to the spigot in a barrel of very fine "old rye," he began to fill it. After drawing several gallons, a friend informed him of his mistake. But it was too late; the whole contents of the sack were saturated with "spirits." Abandoning that one, he picked up another, which was soon filled. Only a few prisoners were captured here, and they escaped, while the men "went through" the stores. After all the men had provided themselves with what their necessities required, orders came to recross the river. In crossing the river the men presented a novel appearance, being completely enveloped in goods, with nothing visible of them but their heads and horses.

After the crossing had been accomplished safely, we moved back from the river one and a half miles, and bivouacked on the Hon. James Mason's farm, and on the road leading to Leesburg. That night three wagons were pressed into service, and our plunder sent back to Fauquier. While the men were loading these wagons, the owner of one of the stores we had gone through, came up to Colonel Mosby, who on certain representations made to him, gave him permission to take from the men all goods that had his mark. Two of the wagons had already started out, which he reported to Colonel Mosby; whereupon, Mosby gave him an order permitting him to proceed to Fauquier County unmolested, and search, and take his goods wherever he found them. A large quantity of his goods were taken out of the lot in camp, and the men turned around and bought them at the owner's own prices, just in the same manner as a person would go into a store to make a purchase. In Fauquier, what goods the merchant found were carried to Middleburg, and sold to the citizens. In the opinion of all rational men, this statement will effectually refute the charge the enemy made against us of being a pack of robbers. The next day the enemy scouted down to the Point, to see what was done. They approached the town very cautiously, and finding no "Johnnies" in the place, they became careless. The officer in command detailed a squad to go up the river to the abutments of a burnt bridge, and reconnoitre.

The eagle eye of Mosby, having from the "lookout" seen them approach the town, he took a few picked men, and reached the river before they did. With him he had a young man named Martin, from King and Queen County, Virginia, who promised to vie with Colonel Mosby in deeds of daring, &c. On the battle-field he was the bravest of the brave, and in the charge his impetuosity knew no bounds. Being a splendid shot, he was always in the front with Colonel Mosby; and when the charge was sounded, his soul seemed fired; and away he would go, frequently ahead of his commander, right into the enemy, firing right and left, every shot telling; and when his ammunition was exhausted, he has been frequently seen using the butt-end of his pistols over the heads of the enemy, and always with telling effect. The keen eye of this young man, as he approached the river, observed in the distance on the opposite side, several of the enemy behind one of the abutments of the burnt bridge. He snatched a Sharp's rifle from one of his companions, and seeking a good position opposite the abutment, he spied a Yankee taking sight at one of his party, while only a few inches of his head could be seen. Colonel Mosby was standing by, when Martin asked if he saw " that fellow on the other side behind the abutment." Before Mosby could reply, the crack of the rifle was heard, and the head suddenly disappeared. The enemy retreated in great haste, Martin mounted his horse, dashed across the river, went to the abutment, and lo! there lay one of the enemy dead, with his gun cocked ready to fire at his Johnny; but another Johnny was too quick for him. The fellow was shot as if the muzzle of the gun had been placed to his head. Martin brought his gun and accoutrements to the Virginia side of the river, and did good service with it afterwards. For this piece of service, Colonel Mosby complimented Martin before the whole command. After this affair the enemy retreated from the river, towards Frederick, Maryland.

CHAPTER XXIV.

<small>MAJOR FORBES "COMES FOR WOOL AND GOES HOME SHORN"—MOSBY'S LIFE SAVED BY TOM RICHARDS—SOLDIERLY BEARING OF MAJOR FORBES.</small>

THE battalion was formed at three o'clock P.M. on the 5th, and moved in the direction of Leesburg, with the view of crossing the Potomac again at Muddy Branch. The battalion, numbering about one hundred and fifty men (the rest having flanked out and gone home), went into camp that night within five miles of Leesburg. At nine o'clock, after all had fed their horses and lain down to sleep, scouts came in and reported that "Leesburg was full of Yankees, who were looking after us." Horses were resaddled in one moment, and mounted. Our present position being considered unsafe, Colonel Mosby moved up across the mountains by a private road to a point one mile above Waterford, and remained there the rest of the night. During the night scouts were sent out to ascertain the strength of the enemy, and who they were. They returned by sunrise next day, and we broke up camp at seven o'clock, going directly to Leesburg. Arriving there at nine o'clock A.M., we found the enemy two hundred and fifty strong, under the command of Major Forbes, of Boston. He had left the place about one hour before, threatening to annihilate Mosby if he came across him, saying that they came out expressly to meet him, and had been looking two days without finding him. While in Leesburg, Colonel Mosby ascertained that they were picked men from three regiments of cavalry stationed at Falls Church, Anandale, and Fairfax Court House, and under the command of Major Forbes, " fighting major," as Colonel Lowell used to call him.

Colonel Mosby determined to follow him up, and, if he could overtake him, to offer him battle, expressing, at the same time, a desire to meet him at or near Mrs. Skinner's, below Aldie, on the Alexandria Turnpike. Meeting with no detention in Leesburg, we moved rapidly to Ball's Mill, on Goose Creek, a great rendezvous for the enemy when scouting up to our Confederacy. Here we expected to meet them. Mosby, disposing his men to the best advantage, waited a few minutes for them. No enemy making their appearance, we struck for the turnpike below Mrs. Skinner's. Companies A and B were sent off, under the gallant Richards, by one road, while Mosby took Companies C and D with him. The turnpike was struck one mile below Mrs. Skinner's, by both squads at the same time. Colonel Mosby, with John Waller and Munson, had preceded his men, and found the enemy feeding their horses at the very place he wanted to meet them, in a large field one mile square. Mosby was seen by the enemy's pickets, who gave the alarm. They soon bridled their horses, and formed in line of battle across the turnpike, before Mosby's men arrived. Mosby, with six men, charged their advanced guard, which fell back to their main column. He then fell back himself, and formed his men in the turnpike. The artillery was then brought up, and one shell fired into their ranks, which broke them. Simultaneous with the firing of the gun, the charge was ordered, and before the enemy could re-form, we were into them. Major Forbes, the bravest Federal officer we ever met, tried to rally his men in the field on the right of the road, three times failing in his efforts. His last effort was a beautiful retreat behind a fence which stretched across the field. Drawing his sabre, he cried, " Rally around your major for the last time, and repulse them." But so impetuous was our charge, that it was beyond a possibility for them to rally. Some, however, did so, and fought gallantly. Our men closed in on them, and a hand-to-hand fight ensued.

It was here that Mosby would have been cut in two by Forbes's sabre, but for the brave Tom Richards, who warded off the blow with his pistol, and received a severe flesh wound on the shoulder, from Forbes's sabre. Forbes, seeing no chances of escape, surrendered like a brave soldier. Then ensued a fight of the most exciting character. The enemy were armed with Spencer's seven-shooters, pistols, and sabres, while we had nothing but pistols; and this compelled us to close in on them. The enemy retreated precipitately by the Braddock Road, pursued by us for six miles, they pouring into us Mr. Spencer's *unpalatable pills* the whole distance, but without injury to any one. The enemy fought like soldiers, and ought to have engaged in a better cause; but when first broken, we would close in on them, and afford them no opportunity to rally.

This was a proud day for Mosby. He had vanquished, in fact annihilated, with one hundred and fifty men, two hundred and fifty men picked out of three regiments for their bravery and fighting qualities, who had been out three days looking for Mosby. Colonel Mosby had one man (Smallwood) killed and three wounded. The enemy lost fifteen killed, including two commissioned officers; on the field, twenty-five wounded and sixty prisoners, including Major Forbes and two commissioned officers. Seventy-five horses were also captured and distributed amongst the men. The wounded were kindly cared for by Mrs. Skinner until next day, when Colonel Lowell came up with ambulances and removed them to camp. Night coming on, we moved up the turnpike, and went into camp. Next morning at sunrise we passed through Middleburg; thence to Piedmont, on the Manassas Gap Railroad, where there was a division of the property, and a detail made to carry the prisoners to Richmond.

Mosby was not unmindful of Tom Richards's endangering his own life to save that of his colonel. The Secretary of War at Richmond had written to Mosby for an officer to go on the Northern Neck to break up the blockade-running carried on in that quarter. Mosby replied he had "none to spare; but the bearer of this is a young man who is every way worthy of any trust or confidence you may be pleased to repose in him." Richards, in due time, presented this to the Secretary of War, who appointed him captain. Men were given him, and he was sent to the Neck, rendering there good service.

In this engagement with Forbes, there were acts of heroism performed, which, but for fear of making invidious distinctions, I would present to my readers. There was one, however, of which I cannot refrain from speaking. It was the conduct of young Martin, who, having his horse shot under him early in the action, pursued the enemy afoot, and at dark returned to camp, mounted on a fine horse, with one prisoner.

CHAPTER XXV.

STRINGENT ORDERS AGAINST PLUNDERING — EARLY'S APPROACH TO WASHINGTON — CONSTERNATION THERE — EXPLOITS OF CHAPMAN — ORGANIZATION OF COMPANY E — THE POTOMAC RECROSSED — A BRILLIANT FEAT.

ON the 12th of July, Captain William H. Chapman, with one hundred men, crossed the Potomac River at Muddy Branch. Having burned the cavalry camp there, he occupied Adamstown. On account of the behavior of the men at Point of Rocks, Captain Chapman issued stringent orders against the men's plundering the stores in this place. Finding no enemy here, he recrossed the Potomac, and returned to Fauquier with a few government horses.

Between the 1st and 18th of July this year, important events had occurred on the soil of Maryland. Generals Early and Breckenridge had crossed the Potomac, dispersed the Union troops and militia under General Wallace at

Frederick City, and were marching triumphantly on Washington. His orders were to only threaten the place; but Early could have captured the city as easily as threaten it; and had General Lee been advised of the strength of the garrison, I am sure he would not have hesitated one moment as to the orders he would have given Early. Almost every available soldier had been sent to Grant; and I am correctly informed, two thousand five hundred regular troops could not have been brought into action. The greatest consternation prevailed in the Capitol of the nation. President Lincoln had fled to Philadelphia; Stanton and the other members of the Cabinet were on a monitor in the Potomac, ready to escape down the river; and our Southern friends confidently expected the Rebels to come in and take the place. Early, however, confined himself to carrying out General Lee's orders. He made a demonstration on their works a mile and a half from the city, threw a few shells into Seventh Street, and retired. Had he pushed on after the engagement at Frederick City, transcended General Lee's orders by going into the city, and destroyed the public buildings and captured some prominent and leading officials, he might have terminated the war. But no: he had executed his superior's order to the letter, and retired without opposition, bringing with him large numbers of horses, mules, cattle, &c., and several thousand prisoners. He recrossed the Potomac below Berlin, and the Blue Ridge Mountains at Snicker's Gap, with his army, sending his prisoners, wagon-trains, and cattle up to Ashby's Gap, to cross Friday night.

On the 18th, we had a meeting at Upperville, and moved off at noon. Early had been pursued, and the enemy's army, under Wright, was already at Snickersville. The afternoon of the 18th, the enemy's cavalry, three thousand strong, under Durfay, dashed into Upperville. It was garrisoned by five hundred men; the rest pressed on up the turnpike to Paris and Ashby's Gap that night, which points they occupied. Camping that night in the woods, next morning we entered Middleburg. Then, Colonel Mosby sent Captain A. E. Richards with Company B, to Fairfax County, to engage a party of the enemy scouting up every day to Thoroughfare Gap; Companies A and D, Captain Montjoy, he took to operate on the grade between Leesburg and Snickersville; while Company C, under William Chapman, went to Ashby's Gap, to operate there.

The enemy had tried to force a passage across the Shenandoah at Castleman's Ferry, but were repulsed with terrible loss. Durfay had likewise attempted a passage of the same river at Berry's Ferry, three times, under a galling fire from Imboden's men behind some light breastworks on the valley side, and fared even worse than Wright did lower down at Castleman's Ferry. Durfay lost five hundred men killed and wounded, and the river was almost dammed up with dead men and horses. Chapman, who was in the Gap, was not idle while this was going on. He was continually firing into and harassing the enemy, picking off one man here, and another there, until Durfay, imagining Early had sent a large force around to attack him in the rear, sounded the retreat. Chapman suddenly concentrating his men (only sixty) dashed between their advance and their picket of sixty men, posted in the Gap at the old Poplar tree, swept them off down the mountain, through Paris, to a safe place beyond

Semper's, with General Durfay and two thousand cavalry after them. Durfay, however, pursued him no farther than Paris, when they moved down the turnpike, and rejoined the army at Snickersville.

Chapman, in this affair, captured forty horses and thirty prisoners; the rest jumped behind the stone fence, and hid until the main column came up. Chapman lost one man, his Orderly Sergeant, who was thrown from his horse, and injured so severely that he died a few days afterwards. Richards, with Company B, did nothing of consequence. The scouting to Thoroughfare Gap had been discontinued. John Atkins, Sam Alexander, Walter Whaley, and two others, while scouting near Union Mills, met with a squad (ten) of the enemy, captured five, including one lieutenant, with their horses, &c. Returning to command, Richards ordered us to return to Fauquier. Mosby, with Companies A and D, captured one hundred and two Infantry, and sent them to Richmond.

On the 28th of this month, Company E was organized, Sam Chapman as Captain, Font Beatty (Mosby's confidential friend), First Lieutenant, Ben Palmer, of Richmond, Third

Lieutenant, and the impetuous Martin, Second Lieutenant, all elected for their daring and fighting qualities. After the organization of Company E, the battalion started for Maryland again. Crossing the Potomac at Nolen's Ferry without opposition, Mosby pushed on to Adamstown, occupied it, and captured twenty prisoners and thirty horses, again refusing to let the men plunder the stores. Recrossing the river with his prisoners, he left Company E, on the Maryland side, to scout and report to him. On their return to the rest of the command at night, Chapman was attacked by the Eighth Illinois Cavalry, and his men retreated in confusion. Lieutenant Beatty, with six men, formed a rear guard, and by charging the enemy and falling back a little, and recharging, succeeded in getting his men across the river, all safe but one, who, being a little tight, fell off his horse and was captured.

Mosby, having got all his men across the Potomac again, moved off the next day to the Valley, crossing the Mountains at Snicker's Gap, and sent William Chapman back to Fauquier with prisoners, and ordered him to bring every man back, with the alternative of going into the regular service. Chapman brought back with him, the next day, thirty men, and met Mosby four miles above Charlestown. Waiting there several hours, and no enemy making their appearance, Mosby ordered his men back to Fauquier. Walter Frankland, our quartermaster, took twenty men with him to thrash wheat in the valley, for the battalion. The enemy, during their occupation of Snicker's Gap, tried to see how much damage and suffering they could bring upon the people in the vicinity of the Gap. Their horses and cattle were turned loose in the cornfields, gardens were destroyed, poultry, pigs, and cows killed, and not a thing left to the helpless people.

On the 6th of August, Mosby took thirty-five men from Company A to Fairfax, and accomplished one of the most brilliant feats of the war. While scouting with two or three men (the rest being hid in the woods) he ran into one hundred and five Yankees, between Fairfax Court House and Fairfax Station, on the Orange and Alexandria Railroad. The enemy, suspecting it was Mosby, mounted their horses and formed in an open field. Mosby sent for his men and charged them. The enemy reserved their fire until he was within forty yards of them. They then opened on him with carbines. This fire was harmless, being too high. After the first volley, seeing none of their foe fall, they broke and retreated in great confusion, with Mosby after them. Ten were killed, including one captain, and twenty prisoners were taken, besides twenty-seven horses, which were brought away; and, strange to say, Mosby and his men sustained no loss. A few hours, however, before the engagement, one man was bushwhacked, receiving a slight wound.

CHAPTER XXVI.

CAPTURES AT BERRYVILLE — NEW UNIFORMS — LIEUTENANT GLASS-
COCK CAPTURES TWENTY MEN — PLANS DEFEATED.

IN compliance with orders, two hundred and fifty men reported at Rectortown, on the 12th of August, for duty. Two mountain howitzers, presented to Colonel Mosby by General Stuart, were taken along for an emergency. They moved off at noon, passing through Snicker's Gap, and fording the Shenandoah River at Castleman's Ferry just at dark. From there our course was directed to the vicinity of Berryville. Concealing the men in the woods, four miles from the town, and one mile from the turnpike leading to Charlestown, Mosby, John Russell, and two others went out to pike to see what was going on. In a few minutes, an ambulance drawn by four mules, with a guard of two men, approached them. Mosby, concluding he might possibly learn something from them regarding the wagon-trains, rode up to them, and before letting them know who he was, inquired how long since his train had passed, and would camp near Berryville. The enemy, regarding him as a Union officer, promptly replied that it had just passed up. Demanding their surrender, and sending them back to the command, he and Russell pushed on to ascertain the whereabouts of the train. One mile from Berryville they found the train in camp, with a guard of one regiment of infantry and five hundred cavalry. The infantry, however, were in Berryville, and the cavalry two and a half miles beyond.

Returning to his men on the morning of the 13th, at daylight, Mosby moved to make the attack. Reaching their encampment at sunrise, just as they were breaking it, he took Company A with him to disperse one hundred infantry at the head of the train; A. E. Richards, with Company B, was to attack the train on the left; Company D supported the artillery, and Company C was to secure the plunder. The signal for attack was the first shot, which fell into a group of teams and men standing about midway of the train. Companies A and B, to reach the point from which they were to attack, were compelled to pass in full view of the train for half a mile, and the artillery a quarter of a mile to two hundred yards of the train for a position. The enemy made no preparations to resist an attack, thinking we were their own men trying to play a trick on them. The artillery fired one shot, which fell short by one hundred yards. Still they all stood gazing at our movement, and moved not a step. Another shot was fired which fell and exploded in their midst. Then came the charge on our side, and the stampede amongst the wagons, some with drivers, others without, they taking refuge behind a stone fence fifty yards from the road. The infantry retreated and sought refuge in a church in the suburbs of Berryville, and from its windows opened a galling fire on Company A, which compelled them to fall back to the train. But few of the wagons escaped. Five hundred mules, one hundred horses, two hundred and twenty-five head of cattle, and two hundred prisoners were brought away.

The train belonged to the Sixth Army

THOMAS W. S. RICHARDS.

Corps, and in it was the baggage of all its officers. There were also two iron chests filled with greenbacks, to pay off a whole corps, and the one hundred days' men, whose time was about expiring. That we did not learn until we had left; and even had we known it before, I doubt very much whether it would have done us any good, for as soon as the attack was made, an officer in charge of the chests threw them out of the wagon on the ground, and there being no powder along to blow them open, they would have been the means of some of our men being captured. Had the boxes remained in the wagon, we would have hitched every mule and horse in the train to it, but that we would have got them out. The wagons were loaded with commissary stores and forage; one hundred of them were burnt. Before the match was applied to the wagons containing the officers' baggage, our men *froze* on the valises, and brought them away; and after our return to Fauquier, the officers of the Sixth Army Corps would have enjoyed seeing our boys *swelling* in their new uniforms, which had been provided for them with so much expense in New York.

In this engagement Mosby lost two killed, (Sergeant Welby Rector, of Company A, and private —— Heddy, of Company B,) and one wounded, Ed Rector, who was wounded slightly, but painfully, in the ankle. The mules were turned over to the Confederate Government, and one hundred and twenty-five head of the cattle were presented to General Lee, for the Army of Northern Virginia.

On the 18th of August, a meeting of the command was held at Rector's Cross Roads, four miles from Middleburg, to go on a raid to the Valley again. At three o'clock the command moved off. Crossing the mountains at Snicker's Gap, we moved on to the Shenandoah River, and halted, while Mosby sent a scout across to see if the road was clear. Returning in the course of an hour, they brought intelligence of two regiments of cavalry encamped a mile and a half from the river, with dismounted men, or infantry pickets out. Mosby, seeing in a moment he could not accomplish anything (that is, if he made a capture, he could not bring it out, Berry's and Castleman's Ferries being strongly guarded), changed his whole plan of operations. Company A he sent to Fairfax County; Company B, down the Shenandoah River, by a mountain road, to Rock Ford, where we crossed into the Valley, under cover of night. Lieutenant Alfred Glasscock, of Company D, took six men, returned to Fauquier, crossed the Blue Ridge at Ashby's Gap, and the Shenandoah at a private ford, penetrated the enemy's lines as far as Strasburg, where he surprised and captured twenty Yankees and twenty horses, and brought them out safe, without loss or injury.

Company A returned without accomplishing anything; and likewise Company B, although it scoured the country as far as Charlestown, without seeing any of the enemy.

The weather being intensely warm, a few days were afforded our jaded horses to recuperate. A meeting was called at Rectortown, and the roll called. Three hundred men, with two pieces of artillery, reported for duty. At noon the men were moved off, Mosby at the head of the column. Mosby had for some time been contemplating a foray on one of the enemy's camps in Fairfax. He now determined, if possible, to carry his plan into execution. Anandale, six miles from Alexandria, was the camp; crossing the Bull Run Mountains at sunset, he pushed on rapidly, under cover of night, to the camp. The enemy, though, through some of their emissaries who were scattered all over the county of Fairfax, had obtained information of Mosby's designs, and to his surprise, at daylight the next morning Mosby found the enemy had sent all their horses to a camp lower down, and the garrison were placed in the stockades, and were waiting our approach.

Finding his plans frustrated, in a measure, by treachery, Mosby determined to make a demonstration notwithstanding; and Captain Montjoy was sent, with a flag of truce, to demand a surrender, with a threat of shelling in case of refusal. Five minutes were allowed the commander of the post to decide. Feeling secure against any attack — successful — in his strongly fortified position, he sent to Mosby the laconic reply, "to shell and be damned." Mosby opened on him with his artillery, commanded by Sam Chapman. The artillery made no impression on the stockades, and hearing of reënforcements on the way from Falls Church, Mosby abandoned the attack, and returned to Fauquier with his command. The officer in command of Anandale, for his *heroism* on this occasion, was promoted to a Colonelship for "*gallant services.*"

CHAPTER XXVII.

MOSBY PROMOTED TO THE OFFICE OF LIEUTENANT-COLONEL.—CHAPMAN AND MONTJOY PUNISH A GANG OF INCENDIARIES.—UNSUCCESSFUL ATTACKS.

THE wonderful success which attended Major Mosby on all his forays on the enemy, had elicited from Generals Lee and Stuart frequent recommendations to the War Department for his promotion. No officer in the Army of Northern Virginia (and there was many a gallant one) had accomplished as much with a brigade of cavalry as Mosby had with his small band of men. With this small squad he kept the enemy in the Valley, and made them *hug* their fortifications around Washington, at Point of Rocks, Berlin, and Harper's Ferry, Maryland, besides extending the arm of protection to the farmers in the counties of Fauquier, Loudon, Prince William, and the upper portion of Fairfax.

Order and respect for private property prevailed all over these counties; and whenever there was the least trespass on private property, whether it was upon Union or upon Southern farmers, by his own men or by other persons, the trespassers were arrested and sent to Richmond, to be tried by court-martial. In consideration of all these services, the President promoted Mosby to the office of lieutenant-colonel, and a merited promotion it was.

A few days after Mosby's return from Fairfax, Captain Sam Chapman of Company E, and Montjoy of Company D, took portions of their companies (sixty men) into the Valley on a raid. When near Berryville, they met a party of the enemy applying the torch to every barn, stable, and out-house in their march, shooting and killing stock in the fields. Innocent women and children and old men were turned out of doors, and their houses and all burnt to the ground. The sight presented to Chapman and his men aroused all the worst passions of the soldier; and there was one general shout of "no quarter!" Chapman and Montjoy, with their sixty men, swept down on the enemy like a whirlwind. Forty were killed on the spot. Thirty-five horses and two prisoners were brought off. The prisoners were sent to Culpepper by a German baron.

On the 28th of August, Colonel Mosby ordered fifty men to meet him in Middleburg. At noon we moved off down the turnpike, passing through Aldie, and bivouacked that night near Mr. Cross's, in Fairfax County. At daylight, the next morning, scouts were started out in all directions, to find *game*. Mosby, hearing a large body of the enemy's cavalry were moving up the turnpike towards Middleburg, took Bob Walker and myself out with him. We went back to within two miles of Aldie, before we learned anything definite as to the strength of the column which had just passed up. There we learned six hundred cavalry and several wagons had gone up one hour before. Deeming it unnecessary to follow them further, we retraced our march to the men who still remained in the woods near Mr. Cross's.

When half way back, on the turnpike, we were met by Bush Underwood and John Sinclair, running for their lives, with one hundred and eighty New York cavalry after them. The whole party were then chased up the turnpike about two miles, when Mosby dodged into the woods, and let the enemy pass. When they disappeared, Mosby returned to the turnpike, and learned " they were going up to reënforce the Eighth Illinois at Middleburg." Refreshing ourselves with a glass of hard cider at Mr. ——'s, Mosby returned to his men. After an hour's rest, he moved us lower down in the county, to the farm of Mrs. Moore. Here we remained in the woods until the afternoon of the next day. We were then divided into three squads; Harry Hatcher, lieutenant of Company A, *alias* Deadly Hatcher, took twelve men; Lieutenant Albert Wren, of Company B, took fourteen men; and the rest were under Mosby.

The intention of Mosby was to take every picket-post around Alexandria that night. The enemy, however, heard we were in the neighborhood, and trebled the strength of their pickets; and instead of six or eight men on duty, there were twenty-five at each post, besides several scouts started out to scatter or capture us. Mosby sent —— Mason, John Dickson, Fred and John Hepkins, to take the post at Falls Church. The attack was before day, but not successful. Mason fell wounded, but escaped to the bushes, under cover of night, and reached Colonel Elgey's, in London County, the next day, having marched forty miles with a ball in his leg. The rest of the party escaped uninjured. Lieutenant Albert Wren and his party were chased out by a scouting-party before they had got even a sight of their work.

Harry Hatcher and Bush Underwood, with their party, had been charged with the duty of taking the post at Lewinsville. Hatcher, with Bush Underwood as guide, had managed to get in sight of his work without being seen by any of their scouts; but unfortunately for us, we were seen by a sergeant, who reported the fact in camp, and a large scouting-party was sent after us. Night coming on, we sought refuge in the thick pines, and remained there until nine o'clock, when the enemy returned to their camp. We then emerged from our hiding-place, and started back for Fauquier, taking in our route Mrs. Swinks', a great rendezvous for Federal officers, expecting to pick up a few of the French gentlemen; unfortunately, none were there that evening.

Lieutenant Hatcher, Bush Underwood, Bally Rowser, and myself were invited into the house by Miss Mattie, Mrs. Swinks' accomplished and amiable daughter, and handsomely entertained. Cold ham, crackers, cheese, preserves, &c., &c., were served in great profusion to the half-starved rebels; and we were half starved, for we had not had a "*square meal*" for three days. As we were leaving the house, Miss Swink called us back, saying she had forgotten something. Stepping up stairs, she returned in a moment with a black bottle covered all over with gold, with the stamp of "old Bourbon" on it in large letters. A Federal captain had presented it to her that afternoon, and she told him at the time she never indulged, but would take it and treat her friends with Mosby the first time they came there. It was opened, and after drinking our hostess' health, we drank that of the Captain too, hoping he would again open his heart soon, and let there be a larger flow of that great panacea.

Miss Swinks' parents were Unionists, but she a most uncompromising Southerner; yet she enjoyed the confidence of the Federal officers in and around Washington and Alexandria, and could pass and repass to Alexandria, Washington, and Georgetown at will; and the members of the "old Forty-third" will always remember her with feelings of gratitude for the offices of kindness she showed them while we occupied Fauquier.

Leaving Mrs. Swinks' at ten o'clock, our faces were once more directed to headquarters. On the road we learned that dismounted men were sent out every night to bushwhack us. Fearing we should run into them, we bivouacked that night at Peacock's, and at daylight the next morning resumed our return to Fauquier.

CHAPTER XXVIII.

BEHAVIOR OF THE ENEMY AT MIDDLEBURG—A BLAZE AMONG MOSBY'S MEN—CAPTAIN SAM CHAPMAN ROUTS THE SIXTH NEW YORK CAVALRY—MOSBY WOUNDED—LIEUTENANT GLASSCOCK IN SHERIDAN'S CAMP.

IN Middleburg the enemy behaved most disgracefully, searching and robbing private houses, and insulting ladies. They nearly pulled the finger off one young lady, Miss Nolen, in their efforts to take a ring. She fought like a *rebel* for it, and kept it, too. The cowardly wretches, however, bruised her arms until they were blue.

One remarkable fact about the enemy's cavalry around Washington and Alexandria was, that of all the scouts they ever made to Mosby's Confederacy, invariably every one was made when Mosby was absent on a raid with his men. How it happened so it is impossible for me to say, and I should like to have some of the Federal officers commanding those troops explain it. I know of no explanation, unless it was to afford their men an opportunity to plunder, and see how much misery they could heap on a people who sympathized with a government which was struggling with the whole world for their dearest rights.

On the 2d day of September, the whole command met at Rectortown. Colonel Mosby took Companies A and B and crossed the Blue Ridge at Snicker's Gap; then taking the road down the Shenandoah River, a march of seven miles brought him to Rock Ford. Hiding his men in the mountains, Mosby, with Captain A. E. Richards and ten men, went on a scout across the river in search of Captain Blaze. Blaze had crossed the river at that ford that morning, had gone up to the stillhouse a few miles from the river, and it was supposed had returned to the valley by another road; but, instead of returning to the Valley from the stillhouse, they took the road up to Snickersville. Reaching there, they learned Mosby had passed through the gap on a raid. Getting on our track and following it up, they found us with horses unsaddled and half the men asleep. Charging us from the rear, they created the greatest consternation amongst the men. Lieutenant Joe Nelson, of Company A, and Horace Johnson, of Company B, rallied fifteen or twenty of the men and charged the enemy, and were driving them back when Nelson unfortunately fell from his horse, dangerously wounded in the thigh. The men no longer tried to keep the enemy at bay, but commenced a disorderly retreat. They were pursued by the drunken foe, and suffered heavily, three being killed and several wounded; but few were taken prisoners. Although these Yankees were drunk, I must say they had more of the instincts of men, and feelings of humanity about them on that day, than any we ever met before. Our wounded they carried to houses in the neighborhood, and requested every attention to be shown to them until removed.

Captain Sam Chapman, with the other squadron, crossed the Blue Ridge at Ashby Gap, and the Shenandoah River at Shepherd's Mill; then directing his course towards Berryville, half a mile below the town, he met the Sixth New York Cavalry, and routed them, killing twenty and capturing thirty horses and thirty prisoners, including two officers. It was a dear capture, though, and made at the expense of some of the brightest ornaments to the battalion, — Lieutenant Frank Fox, of Company C, and Jarmain, of Company E. Fox was one of the bravest of the brave, and by his genial nature and social qualities, had won the confidence and heart not only of Mosby, but of the whole command. His loss was serious, and much deplored. His horse carried him into the midst of the enemy, where he was wounded seriously in the arm, and taken prisoner. He was kept in a private house for three days, and then sent to Harper's Ferry in an oxcart. At the Ferry his arm was amputated, not from necessity, but to render him unfit for future service, should he survive the operation. He lingered only three days, when a merciful God snatched him from the hands of his torturers. Jarmain, although a new member, had, by his manly bearing and unflinching courage, gained the confidence and esteem of all, and was looked upon as a rising star of the Forty-third. Clay Adams, who fell mortally wounded in this engagement, was as brave a soldier as ever drew a sabre. Exempt from military duty by disability (being deaf), he entered the service as a private soldier, and fought with a *vim* that would have been creditable to the heroes of old. He was shot through the sides, by which the whole lower portion of the body was paralyzed. The enemy carried him to a neighbor's house, and were kindly treating him. John Russell, Sidney Ferguson, and one or two others crossed the river in the night, went to the house, and brought him away, although the house was strongly guarded. He was brought the next day to his father's, in Paris, where he lingered for six months. His death was lamented by all who knew him.

Mosby, with his squad, returned with twelve mules and five prisoners, which he had captured near Charlestown. Nothing of any consequence was done for nearly two weeks. Colonel Mosby, with two men, Walter Whaley and —— Love, started on a scouting expedition to Fairfax, and when in the neighborhood of Centreville, they were attacked by a party of seven of Colonel Lowell's men. Two of the enemy were killed, two wounded, and the other three took to flight. In the engagement Mosby received a painful wound in the groin of the leg. After the enemy's retreat, he was brought by Whaley and Love to the White Plains, where his wound was dressed, and the next day he started for his father's, in Amherst County. Captain William H. Chapman, of Company C, being senior officer, assumed command. During Mosby's absence, scouting in small squads was all the rage.

Lieutenant Alfred Glasscock took ten men, crossed over in the valley, entered Sheridan's camps, and rode through them as Provost Guard, with orders to take all men found absent from their camps, to Sheridan's headquarters. Glasscock met fifteen men and officers, mounted them on the finest horses in the camp, and, instead of carrying them to Sheridan's headquarters, he started for Mosby's headquarters in Fauquier. On the way, when near Berry's Ferry, three surgeons were met. The usual halt and questions passed. Glasscock, satisfying the surgeons he was "all right," advanced to where they were, and after a few inquiries where they had been, and if they had seen or heard of any rebels, ordered them to fall in and follow him. The surgeons complimented Glasscock very highly for his skill in the management of this affair, and complied with his order with very good grace. Glasscock reached Fauquier with eighteen horses and prisoners, without firing a shot, or having a man injured.

CHAPTER XXIX.

SUCCESSFUL TRIPS OF LIEUTENANT RUSSELL AND COMPANIONS — THE WRITER'S VISIT TO RICHMOND — DECLINES URGENT INVITATIONS TO MAKE HIS HOME IN THE INTRENCHMENTS — MOSBY ATTACKS THE ENEMY AT SALEM — VARIOUS CAPTURES, ETC.

LIEUTENANT JOHN RUSSELL, of Clark County, —— Magner, of Mississippi, Dr. Lowers, of the Valley, and Ab Suttle crossed the Shenandoah River every night, attacked picket-posts, and harassed the enemy at every point in the Valley, giving them no rest night or day. Every trip they made was a successful one, in securing prisoners and horses. Lieutenant John Russell established daily communication with General Sheridan's headquarters at Winchester. Daily Baltimore papers (the "Gazette" and "American") were received in Paris at nine o'clock the night after they were issued.

Mosby being still absent, on account of his wound, large numbers of the men availed themselves of the opportunity (*business* being very dull) of getting a short furlough, to go home, and take with them what had been captured during the summer campaign in Maryland and the various camps. I availed myself of the opportunity, and paid a flying visit of two days to Richmond. I met there my Captain, A. E., and Tom Richards, and also John Atkins, of County Cork, Ireland, who had crossed the Atlantic " to join Mosby." Mr. Atkins was a younger brother of Captain Atkins (now Lord ——) of General Elzey's staff.

The day after my arrival in Richmond, Fort Harrison was taken by the enemy, and the greatest alarm prevailed in the city. The town bell was rung, militia called out, and guards placed at every corner, to take up furloughed soldiers and officers (with which the city was filled) to go to the intrenchments, and check the advance of the enemy. After being picked up on the street, they were marched by a guard to what was called the Soldier's Home, there organized into companies, and then marched out to the army. Atkins and myself were amongst the fortunate ones they desired to go out; but having completed our arrangements to leave the city the next morning for Fauquier, our Captain had no idea of spending the remainder of the campaign in those agreeable places, " the intrenchments;" and having learned the art of flanking pretty well with Mosby, I determined to apply it in this instance. I got to my room safe, and coming out of it to see my Captain at the Spottswoods, was picked up the second time. I flanked out the second time, and reached my room. While looking out of the window, I observed most of the guards were dressed in citizen's dress; and having an old musket and cartridge-box in my brother's office, I conceived the idea of playing guard; so shouldering my musket, and adjusting the cartridge-box, I went forth in quest of men to go out and defend their Capitol. Every man was made to show his papers. The first person I ran against was my old comrade-in-arms, Charlie Hall, who had likewise got into the same trouble as myself. I took him into custody, and he took me by turns; by that means we managed to get through our little business, and have everything ready to leave by the morning train, with my Captain, A. E. Richards. My reasons for acting in this manner I considered the very best. I thought I could do my country more good in Fauquier, with the great partisan; besides, I had no idea of spending the fall in the intrenchments.

. Atkins pursued a different plan, and much bolder. At the armory, when handed his musket, he refused to take it, stating his reasons to the officer commanding the company, and to General Barton. They " couldn't see it," but marched him back to the Soldier's Home. He, however, was released the next day, through the intercession of Captain Ed Hudson, of General Elzey's Staff, and formerly of the Prussian army. That night orders were issued to allow no one to leave the city. Guards were stationed at daylight at every corner in the city, to pick up men who could not show proper papers. Having procured passports to leave the city the day before, and before the enemy made this movement on our lines, I had no difficulty in reaching the depot, although my pass was examined very critically by at least twelve soldiers. At the depot, agreeably to arrangements, I met Captain A. E. Richards. We left Richmond at nine o'clock, and reached Gordonsville at the usual time. There we found Mosby, returning to his command. He and Richards went by rail to Culpepper, where their horses were, and I by Madison Court House, Washington, Rappahannock County, and Barber's Cross Roads, reaching Fauquier in three days.

Colonel Mosby had not entirely recovered from his wound, yet he resumed his seat in the saddle immediately. On reaching Fauquier, he found the enemy coming up the Manassas Gap Railroad through Thoroughfare Gap, in strong force of Infantry and Cavalry. They occupied the Plains and Salem. A meeting of the whole command was ordered at Piedmont. Mosby attacked them at Salem, with two hundred and fifty men, and drove them back to the Plains, and burned the depot there, with a large quantity of stores, &c. In the engagement Mosby made a narrow escape with his life. His horse, stumbling, fell on him, and sprained his ankle. Before he could get up, a Federal soldier galloped over him, and fired as he passed; but a wise Providence changed the direction of the ball, and it missed him.

The enemy receiving reënforcements at the Plains, Mosby fell back to Piedmont, without losing a man. At Piedmont he rested his men one day. In the meanwhile the enemy occupied Rectortown, and fortified themselves. Two thousand constituted the garrison. On the west side of Rectortown is a range of high hills, overlooking the town. The enemy having no cavalry, Mosby determined to shell them out of the place, if possible. Concealing one half of his men in the woods, with the other half he took a position on one of these hills on Mrs. Rawling's farm, and opened on them with two pieces of artillery (one gun and a howitzer). Skirmishers were thrown out. The enemy retreated, but soon rallied and sought refuge under their intrenchments, from which retreat they could not be drawn. Several, however, were killed and wounded. After an hour's shelling, our ammunition gave out, and Mosby ordered us to fall back and renew the attack next day.

Promptly at eight o'clock, all met at Joe Blackwell's, two miles from Rectortown. With the assistance of glasses, the enemy could be seen, working like beavers, strengthening their works. The attack was to be renewed at nine o'clock. Mosby and his men became impatient for the fray, which was delayed by the artillery's not coming up. It finally reached us at three o'clock, and Mosby attacked them in their fortifications. They started off a train of cars down the railroad, with one thousand Infantry on it. Mosby attacked it; but by the late arrival of the artillery the train was lost. The enemy, however, were driven from it, and it flew down the railroad to Salem. The enemy retreated across the fields towards Salem, pursued by Mosby and his men. They took a position on a mountain to the right of Salem, with a high stone fence at its base, and could not be dislodged, on account of the natural strength of their position. Mosby formed his men in line of battle, and opened on them with his artillery, but without effect.

While the enemy were in this position, Albert Wren, Bully Rowser, John Iden, Dr. Sowers, Sidney Ferguson, and Reub Triplett distinguished themselves by their bravery in charging up the mountain to the enemy, and discharging their pistols at them.

Mosby, finding he could not dislodge the enemy, retired at sunset and disbanded his men. The enemy that night were reënforced by two thousand five hundred cavalry from Washington and Muddy Branch. The next day we met at Freds, on the top of one of the spurs of the Blue Ridge. One hundred of us started down the mountain, under Captain William H. Chapman, to engage a force of about one hundred and fifty of the enemy, at Mrs. Shacklett's, half a mile from Piedmont. Having got in the rear of Mrs. Shacklett's house, Lieutenant John Russell, who had gone ahead to see if the country was clear, suddenly came dashing down the mountain on the opposite side of Crooked Run, warning us of our danger, and telling us to fall back. No sooner had we seen him than the brow of the mountain was black with the enemy, the foremost about ten rods behind Russell. The enemy complimented us with three rounds, when we retired. Anticipating our attack on the party at Mrs. Shacklett's, they had sent a force of three or four hundred around and concealed them under this mountain to attack us in the rear, should we bite at the bait they had set for us; but the keen eye and sagacity of Russell frustrated all their nice-laid plans.

While this was going on near Piedmont,

the enemy, concluding all our men had left the country, except those with Chapman, sent a party of sixteen from Rectortown, *via* Upperville and Paris, with dispatches to General Sheridan in the valley. Their arrival in Upperville, in such a small squad, was a surprise to all. Captain Montjoy being in the neighborhood and hearing of them, sent John Thomas, John Horn, Ab Fox, James Keith, and two others, who followed them through Ashby's Gap and attacked them at the tollgate, between the gap and the river. Nine were captured without making any resistance; the other seven dismounted and fled to the mountains, and, getting lost, came down in the evening to Paris and gave themselves up. Sixteen horses and the dispatches were secured. The dispatches, being in cipher, were sent to Richmond, and the character of them never known.

The morning after this, thirty-five men of Company B met Captain A. E. Richards at Paris, and started on a raid to the valley, crossing at Ashby's Gap, and the Shenandoah River at Island Ford. When near Strasburg Richards attacked fifty cavalrymen and one ambulance belonging to General Sheridan's headquarters. The enemy were routed; six were killed, including Sheridan's chief quartermaster; twenty-eight horses and twelve prisoners were taken. The ambulance, also, was captured with contents, including valuable papers, giving reports of the number of cavalry and artillery horses &c., &c.; these were sent to Richmond.

CHAPTER XXX.

UNITED STATES MAIL-TRAIN CAPTURED — "GOING THROUGH" THE PASSENGERS — CAPTURE OF MOSBY'S ARTILLERY — TRAINS THROWN OFF THE TRACK — GENERAL AUGER ARRESTS FIVE CITIZENS — CRUELTY.

HARRY HEATON of Company D, one of the valley scouts, came in and informed Mosby of a fine opening in the valley on the Baltimore and Ohio Railroad. Mosby ordered a meeting for the next day, the 13th of October, at Bloomfield, in Loudon County, a small village five miles from Snicker's Gap. Seventy men reported for duty. At noon the mountains were crossed at Snicker's Gap, and the Shenandoah River at Castleman's Ferry. Pushing on through Cabletown, night overtook the party at Dr. William's, in Jefferson County. Here Colonel Mosby, the officers, and a few men, were very hospitably entertained by the doctor and his accomplished daughters. At nine o'clock the march was resumed. The scout having learned the hour the train was due at Duffield Station, the railroad was struck half an hour before it was due, obstructions were placed on the track at the depot, and all awaited anxiously the arrival of the train.

In due time the express came lumbering to the station and stopped. A guard was placed over the engine and the men entered the cars. Two paymasters were found with one hundred and seventy thousand dollars of Government funds. The greenbacks were confiscated, and started out to Fauquier by Lieutenants Briscoe, Grogan, of Company D, and two men. Some of the men commenced " going through " the passengers. One Southerner was put through the mill by being relieved of a fine watch, which Mosby found out, and made the fellow return it, through him, to the owner in Baltimore. A number of the men exchanged overcoats, hats, gloves, &c. with the passengers. One hog-drover, who was returning to his home in the West, from Washington, where he had drawn his money for a lot of hogs sold to the Government, was relieved of the burden of five thousand dollars. John Horn, who commenced going through a big Prussian officer, was seized by the throat and choked until his tongue hung out, but was extricated from his perilous situation by Puryear's dispatching his assailant. The cars were destroyed, and Mosby started back with twenty prisoners and fifteen horses, without loss. The following is General Lee's dispatch to the Secretary of War in Richmond: —

ARMY OF NORTHERN VIRGINIA,
October 16, 1864.

On the 14th instant Colonel Mosby struck the Baltimore and Ohio Railroad at Duffield Station, destroyed a United States mail-train, consisting of locomotive and ten cars, and secured twenty prisoners and fifteen horses. Among the prisoners are two paymasters, with one hundred and sixty-eight thousand dollars Government funds.

R. E. LEE, *General, &c.*

The money was divided equally amongst the men, officers and men sharing alike. Mosby, however, refused to take a cent.

During Colonel Mosby's absence on this raid, the enemy captured his artillery, through the treachery of one of his men, who, for a purse of gold, told them where it was. When the enemy occupied the Manassas Gap

Railroad, Captain Franklin, commanding the artillery, imprudently hid it in the Cobblar Mountain, instead of the Blue Ridge. Lunsford, the traitor, told them where it was. The enemy surrounded the mountain in the night, with a large force of cavalry, and sent two hundred dismounted men up into the mountain to its place of concealment. These captured it, and the men guarding it. The loss of our artillery was a serious one, but did not terminate our forays on the enemy. The enemy, however, made a great fuss and hurrah over its capture, and also that of one wagon-train. Mosby had two wagons at this time; and I know, from my own personal knowledge, they did not get these, for no Federal soldier was ever in the Blue Ridge Mountains where they were hid; and in April, 1865, when I left Fauquier County, the same wagons were there then; so General Augur was mistaken about a wagon-train being captured belonging to us. If his men captured any wagons that night, they *captured* them from the citizens.

The enemy having fortified themselves at Rectortown, the Plains, and Salem, with a large force at Piedmont, scoured Fauquier

County, with the view of driving us out of the country. All the men except those living in and right under the mountains changed their boarding-houses to the southern side of the railroad. Lieutenants K., S., and Y., with a few picked men, amused themselves by tearing up the railroad. Lieutenant K. threw a train of cars off the track between Thoroughfare Gap and Gainesville in the night, killing and wounding several, and smashing up the locomotive and cars. Lieutenants S. and Y. placed torpedoes in the road between Piedmont and Markham. One exploded, and blew a cavalryman and horse to pieces. That stopped their scouting up to Front Royal.

To prevent a repetition of these annoyances, General Augur ordered the arrest of five of the most prominent citizens in the county. The victims of Augur's wrath were Messrs. Jamison, Albert and Samuel Ashby (three brothers, and uncles to the lamented and renowned Turner Ashby), Benjamin Triplett, and another citizen, all old men. These old men were dragged from their beds and the bosoms of their families in the dead hour of night, carried to Rectortown, and made to ride in the front car, to keep us from throwing the trains off the track. Providence, however, relieved Mr. Jamison Ashby from the hands of his persecutors. While sleeping with his neighbors and old friends on the floor of the car one night, he was shot in the head by a guard without any provocation whatever. He was carried to a hospital in Alexandria, and his friends were not only prevented from seeing him and showing him some attention, in alleviating his sufferings, and supplying his wants, but the authorities absolutely refused his daughter the privilege of simply seeing him, at a time, too, when he was in the very throes of death; and the almost heart-broken girl was compelled to return to her home in Fauquier, without ever again in this world gazing upon the face of an affectionate and doting father. This is a sad tale, my readers, and may appear to some as being exaggerated, but it is true. If any one questions the statement, let him visit Fauquier, and inquire of parties who witnessed the deed.

CHAPTER XXXI.

TOO MUCH OF A GOOD THING — TREACHERY — TOO MUCH OF A GOOD THING AGAIN — CAPTAIN FRANKLAND FAILS TO "MAKE HIS JACK."

A FEW days after Colonel Mosby's return from the Valley, he led about two hundred men to Fairfax, to attack a train of two hundred wagons at Burk's Station, on the Orange and Alexandria Railroad. Each wagon was guarded by three negro soldiers. Fifty of these wagons would go out at a time, and were engaged in hauling wood to the depot. We arrived there, however, one hour too late; the wagons and niggers had gone into camp, and six hundred infantry in wagons, were almost too much of a good thing for two hundred cavalry, armed with nothing but pistols; and Mosby concluded to let them rest for another time.

From Burk's Station we went down to Billy Goodwin's tavern, on the turnpike, some ten miles from Alexandria. Meeting with little or no encouragement there, Mosby moved us lower down, in sight of Anandale. Two men were sent to take the picket, and draw the garrison out. One prisoner was taken, the other retreated to camp. The garrison, however, declined to come out. Night approaching, Companies A, B, C, and E, were sent back to Fauquier. Company D, Captain Montjoy, was sent to Falls Church, to capture two hundred cavalry and two stores. Bush Underwood was the guide, and but for the treachery of a citizen, named Reed, Montjoy would have made a clean sweep of the place. The pickets had been flanked, and our men in their camp and at the stables, leading out the horses, when this Union citizen (a spy), gave the alarm by blowing a horn, as we were going into the camp. The men, not suspecting anything, paid no attention to it, but thought somebody was going out a 'possum hunting, though no barking of dogs was heard.

The enemy had taken a position behind some breastworks, and when our men commenced leading out the horses, a volley was fired into them. Lieutenant Glasscock rode out a few paces in the direction the firing came from, and told them to stop firing into their own men. The reply he received was another volley. Thinking prudence the better part of valor, he retired. Passing Reed's house, the boys found out what the blowing of the horn meant, and shot Reed. Had it not been for Reed, the enemy would have been spared the trouble and expense of trying that notorious character Charlie Been, a deserter from Mosby. We regretted exceedingly that we were compelled to leave him and Yankee Davis undisturbed in their slumber in the store at Falls Church that night, with their sable companions. Three negroes, however, were killed, five prisoners taken, and ten horses brought off. Montjoy sustained neither loss nor injury.

On the 22d of October, 1864, a meeting of the command was held at Bloomfield. Very near four hundred men were present, the largest number ever out. We crossed the mountains at Snicker's Gap, and the Shenandoah river at Castleman's Ferry about dusk. That night we camped near Summit Point, and next morning resumed our march at sunrise.

Colonel Mosby took ten men (Sam Alexander, John Russell, John Dickson, Fred Hipkins and others), and went on a scouting expedition, the command following. When on the turnpike between Winchester and Martinsburg, near Mrs. Allen's, six miles from Winchester, he fell in with General Durfay and twenty-five cavalry (Durfay riding in an ambulance), being the advance guard, consisting of three thousand infantry. Fourteen pieces of artillery, and five hundred cavalry, to a train of one thousand wagons. Mosby captured the General, one staff officer, and four privates; the rest retreated to the main column. Russell and Sam Alexander followed them up, but were obliged to retreat or rather get out as fast as they went in. Mosby then came back to the command, threw himself at the head of the First Squadron, Companies A and B, and commenced charging the train. Their cavalry ran off; but their infantry (Zouaves) formed in line of battle, and opened on us with two pieces of artillery. We fell back under cover of a piece of woods and a hill. The enemy parked the wagons, and posted some of their infantry behind and in them, but did not advance. Mosby was in fine spirits, and riding along the column in front of Company B, cried out, —

"Well, ———, which would you rather have, — the General or the wagons?"

"Both," replied ———.

Just then a shell exploded near the Colonel, which terminated the colloquy, and we moved off towards Fauquier.

The battalion dividing below Berryville, the Second Squadron, with Chapman, re-crossed the Shenandoah river at Berry Ferry, and passing through Ashby's Gap, proceeded to Markham, Fauquier County, to watch the movements of the enemy on the Manassas Gap Railroad. The First Squadron, under command of Captain Frankland, of Company F, crossed the Shenandoah river, at Castleman's Ferry; thence through Snicker's Gap to a point (Mum's) between Rectortown and Middleburg, in the hope of intercepting some small scouting-parties of the enemy. After we had lain in the woods watching for them all day, and had neither seen nor heard anything of them, orders came from Captain Richards to disband and go home.

On the 29th of October, Colonel Mosby

ordered a meeting, at Middleburg, of a portion of the command. Lieutenant Wren, with fifteen men, reported, and found the Colonel had gone. From there we pushed on to Carter's Mill. Reaching there, we learned Mosby had just left, without stopping. Getting track of him, we pushed on and overtook his party in the woods one mile and a half from the Mill. Lieutenant Harry Hatcher, of Company A, riding up to us, told us to rest our horses; that two hundred Yankees had just started out from Rectortown, scouting, and that he and Colonel Mosby had been watching them.

Orders soon came to *mount our horses.* The party with Mosby coming up, our number was swelled to one hundred and ten men. Learning the enemy were at Hatcher's Mill, on the Alexandria turnpike, we pressed on in that direction, in high glee, and found them dismounted and feeding their horses. Deeming it hazardous to attack them then, we waited in the woods until they resumed their march, and followed them on until we reached Henry Dulaney's house, about one mile from Upperville. In the meanwhile Mosby left us in charge of Captain Frankland, while he went on the opposite side of the turnpike, at Green Garden Mills, to see Captain A. E. Richards, who had just returned from scouting in the Valley.

Frankland having given up the office of Quartermaster of the battalion, to take command of Company F, a short time before, thought it an excellent opportunity to make his "*Jack.*" The Yankees, knowing we were after them and in that neighborhood, drew up in line of battle in three columns behind a ditch four feet wide, with a six-rail fence over that. The centre numbered about one hundred men, with columns of fifty men on either flank, and were patiently awaiting an attack from us. Frankland, brave and impetuous, could not resist the temptation, although he had received orders just to watch them, and nothing more. He determined to attack the enemy at all hazards. Riding back to his men, he divided them into two squadrons; the first, with forty-five men, being parts of Companies A and B, commanded by the gallant Wren; the Second Squadron, numbering sixty-five men, was commanded by Lieutenant Grogan, of Company D. The First was to charge the enemy, and the Second to support us.

Having formed in fours, and all things being ready, orders came to charge. On we dashed, Wren at the head, over the hill with a yell with which the very mountains in the distance rung. Charging up to within twenty yards of the foe, and seeing their strong position, we looked back for our supports. None being in view, the men began to waver. The enemy, appreciating our position, fired one volley, and then charged through a gate, pouring into the little squad a deadly fire from their Spencer rifles. No assistance coming up, a precipitate retreat was commenced. Our loss in killed, wounded, and prisoners, was heavier than in any previous engagement during the war. Four men were killed, and ten captured. Among the killed was John Atkins, of County Cork, Ireland, and brother of Captain Atkins, late of General Elzey's staff, but now Lord ———.

No higher compliment could be paid to a brave soldier than that paid by Mosby to the noble patriot, as he lay stretched on his bier in Henry Dulaney's house. Some one came in the room while the Colonel was there, and commenced explaining the part played in the affair by certain officers. The Colonel replied, pointing to the dead body of Atkins, —

"There lies a man I would not have given for a whole regiment of Yankees."

John Atkins left home, friends, wealth, and position, and came three thousand miles to fight for a cause which every true Irishman holds most dear. He was brave as he was generous. He knew not what danger was. Fearless as a lion, he was gentle in his manners as a lamb. How touching are those last words he spoke while pouring out his heart's blood at the foot of the shrine of liberty: "Oh, my mother! my poor mother!" He was a man of fine education and most agreeable manners, and enjoyed the esteem and confidence of the whole command. A neat coffin was furnished by his friends, and he was buried in the cemetery at Paris. Mosby, who stood in Captain Richards' front, and witnessed the charge of Companies A and B, complimented Lieutenant Wren very highly for his gallantry on the occasion, in his having displayed all the qualities of a good soldier.

Captain A. E. Richards, the evening of this disaster, had just returned from scouting in the Valley, with only eight men. He was eminently successful, having captured twenty horses and prisoners without loss.

CHAPTER XXXII.

CAPTAIN BRASHER'S EXPEDITION INTO THE CONFEDERACY — GENERAL POWELL'S RAID — RETALIATION — EFFECTS OF RETALIATION — CASE OF ROBERT HARKOVER.

ABOUT this time there appeared in the Valley another conspicuous character, Captain Brasher, alias Blazer, whom the authorities at Washington had selected from their whole army for his bravery and daring, and sent to the Valley, with one hundred men selected by him from their cavalry, and distinguished for their fighting qualities, to "clean out Mosby." Captain Brasher made Cabletown his headquarters. His first act was a proposition to Mosby to take fifty of his men, and whip one hundred of Mosby's best and tried men. Mosby took no notice of his challenge, but bided his time.

In the meanwhile, Brasher, with his men, with a degree of boldness and daring unprecedented in the cavalry of the Army of the

Potomac, made frequent forays into *our Confederacy*, and scoured the Blue Ridge Mountains from Harper's Ferry to Ashby's Gap; which was something no other Federal officer had ever done, unless he had a brigade or a division of cavalry with him. In those expeditions he did nothing very damaging to us, except here and there picking up a Mosbyite and a horse or two. One circumstance which distinguished Brasher and his men above all other Union soldiers that raided into that country, was the respect he and they paid to citizens and private property. The consequence was, his visits were not looked upon with that feeling of dread that was inspired by the raids of other parties.

But we must leave Captain Brasher for a little while, and see what was doing at Rectortown, on the Sunday following. The enemy had left the Manassas Gap Railroad, taking with them all the iron rails and even clamps. Colonel Mosby started on Sunday with two hundred men for Prince William County to Gainesville. Crossing the Bull Run Mountains by a private road, we camped that night on the other side of them. At daylight we moved down to the woods on Mr.

Pickett's farm near Gainsville, and remained there all day. Scouts were sent out to draw the enemy's cavalry away from the railroad. Not being able to get them out, Colonel Mosby ordered Lieutenant Hatcher, with Company A, to a point near Centreville; and the rest of the men, under Lieutenant Grogan, to St. John's Church, near Sudley. There we remained until next day at noon, when orders came to disband and go home, returning by way of Hopewell Gap and the Plains. Hatcher returned without doing anything.

During our absence on this raid, General Powell, with two thousand five hundred cavalry, and four pieces of artillery, made a raid into the Confederacy by way of Front Royal, Linden, Markham, Piedmont, Rectortown, Upperville, and Paris, stealing, in their route, all the stock, cattle, and poultry they could find, and returned to their camp by Ashby's Gap and the Shenandoah River, at Berry's Ferry. The day after Mosby's return from Prince William, he took twenty men to the Valley, and captured seventeen Federals, with their horses, near Winchester. These prisoners belonged to Custar's cavalry, and participated in the shooting and hanging of our men in Front Royal, in the month of September.

Returning to Fauquier with his prisoners, Mosby called a meeting of the men at Rectortown. The prisoners were drawn up in a line, and all drew to see which should be hung in retaliation for those hung and shot in Front Royal, amongst whom were some of the most respectable citizens of Fauquier. One was Anderson, a justice of the peace, visiting at Markham. A short time before that bloody affair, the same brigade hung, at Sandy Hook, Mr. Willis, a Baptist preacher, and a member of the Forty-third. This was done in retaliation, they said, for one of their men whom Chancellor killed.

The history of that case is this: A short time before one of their numerous raids into and through that country, they sent a man ahead to find out who had fine stock, and where they hid it. This fellow represented himself to the farmers as a Confederate soldier, escaped from prison. Some of our men who were travelling through that portion of the country, hearing of him, concluded he was nothing more nor less than a spy. He was sought out, and found at Mr. Chancellor's. Being questioned as to his business, &c., his true character was found out. He was then taken out and shot. A few days after this, a large column of the enemy made a raid through there, and, hearing of this, burned Mr. Chancellor's house, in retaliation for the deed. Not satisfied with that, on their return, Willis was overtaken, and hung for the same thing. For these outrages and violations of all the laws of war, this scene was being enacted at Rectortown. One lieutenant and six privates drew black balls, one of the lucky ones being a newsboy, who had no connection with the army except in vending newspapers to the soldiers, and in no way connected with those that did the hanging. Mosby threw his name out, and another drawing, to make up the seven, was held. The number being now complete, the unfortunate and doomed men were placed under guard, and started back to the Valley, to pay the penalty for their atrocious deeds. In the Valley Montjoy was met, returning with some prisoners. The lieutenant being a Mason (as Montjoy was one), he was exchanged for a private, and the lieutenant went a prisoner to

Richmond, instead of to the gallows. The night being very dark three escaped, but four were hung in sight of the enemy's camp. They were amazed, the next morning, to see their companions in arms dangling in the air.

The next day Mosby wrote to General Sheridan, explaining the reasons which compelled him to adopt this summary and disagreeable method of checking their treatment of his men, and hoped he would never be obliged to do it again; but that if he or General Custar persisted in treating his men in that manner, he was ready to fight them under the black flag. Mosby then stated to him the number of his (Sheridan's) men he had taken prisoners of war, who were kindly treated, and how many he (Sheridan) had captured of his; and if he, with those facts staring him in the face, continued that system of fighting, he would be greatly the loser, and the responsibility of his (Mosby's) course would rest on his (Sheridan's) shoulders.

General Sheridan would not reply to Mosby, or recognize him as an officer in the Confederate Army, but wrote to General Early, then commanding in the Valley, that he had received a communication from Mosby, and that what had been done to (Mosby's) men, was done entirely without his knowledge and authority, and that hereafter Colonel Mosby's men would be treated as prisoners of war.

This hanging had the desired effect. It convinced the enemy how terribly in earnest we were, and that we were entitled to the same privileges that regular soldiers were entitled to. Before this, General Sheridan's and Kilpatrick's Cavalry would offer our men every species of indignity. Instead of having a guard placed over them while awaiting transportation to prison, they were invariably thrown into loathsome jails and dungeons in Warrenton, Winchester, and Martinsburg. At Point Lookout, Johnson's Island, Fort McHenry, Fort Delaware, Camp Chase, and other prisons, we were special objects of insult, torture, and bad treatment. One brave soldier, Robert Harrover, of Washington City, whom they captured in Fairfax, on a scouting-party with Frank Williams, and who the enemy imagined was behind every pine-tree and little bush in Fairfax, with his unerring rifle, was carried to Washington and tried for his life by the Military Commission, "For leaving Washington City after he had been enrolled, and attaching himself to a band of guerillas."

Bob stood his trial, and the night after his condemnation to the Albany Penitentiary for fourteen years, took French leave. Confined in the third story of the Old Capitol Prison, in the dead hour of night he tore up his bed-clothes, and made a rope by which he let himself down to the pavement, and escaped, although the sentry fired at him. The night being very dark, he quickly disappeared, and sought the house of a friend in the city, who provided him with a suit of citizen's clothes. Sallying out the next morning, he passed through Georgetown and Rockville as a member of the Sanitary Commission, bargaining for poultry and supplies for the hospitals. Beyond Rockville he overtook a party of five Marylanders, going South. All being provided with pocket-pistols, they took a picket post, and mounting themselves, pushed on rapidly to the Potomac, and crossed over into Virginia, near Leesburg, and reached the *Confederacy*, after eleven months' imprisonment.

CHAPTER XXXIII.

ESCAPES FROM PRISON — HALL'S ESCAPE — MAGNER'S ESCAPE — ELIMINATION OF SKULKERS — MONTJOY LEARNS SOMETHING ABOUT BRASHER.

DURING this year, 1864, no less than thirty of our men escaped from prison and the guards over them. Charlie Hall, who was a prisoner of Colonel Cole's, and was awaiting transportation to prison at Harper's Ferry, obtaining a Federal overcoat, asked of the guard permission to go to Colonel Cole's headquarters. Instead of going to Colonel Cole's headquarters, he walked out of camp uninterrupted, and reported at Mosby's the next day.

Magner, of Mississippi, was captured in Paris in the night, by taking the enemy for our own cavalry. He was carried to Harper's Ferry a prisoner. Having on a very fine uniform of the Confederate gray, he exchanged it with a Jessie scout for a Federal uniform,

While waiting for transportation to Camp Chase, a large body of troops passed through Harper's Ferry, to reënforce Sheridan in the Valley. At a moment when he was not watched closely, he fell into the column as a common soldier, limping, as if wearied with his march. His *comrades* asked him where his gun was. "In the wagon," replied Magner, and passed on, without attracting any further notice. Watching his chances to escape, he straggled, and sought refuge in the mountains, where he remained all night. Next day he was discovered by a scouting-party, who gave him chase. Jumping down an embankment of fifty feet, which dislocated his shoulder, he plunged into the Shenandoah, swam across with one arm, and was free once more. The next day he reached Fauquier.

On the 11th of November, an inspection of the battalion was held at Rectortown. Five hundred men reported to their names at roll-call. This inspection was held at the request of Mosby. A large number of men had connected themselves with the battalion, whose names were on the rolls of the regular army, and who, thinking to shirk military duty, came up and joined the Forty-third. They were a set of men who very seldom went on a raid; and when they did go, and there was any fighting or horses captured, would lag behind, and when it was all over, would lead the horses out, take the greenbacks from the prisoners, and when near their homes would *flank out* with a horse, and never come up to a division of the property. In that way they lived. This kind of men Mosby did not want, and would not have; and he adopted this method of getting them together with the determination of sending them to Richmond, to be put in the trenches.

Captain Meade, of General Early's staff, was the inspecting officer. The names of these men had been previously obtained from the captains of the companies. When their names were called, and they appeared before the Colonel and Inspector, they were relieved of the equipments furnished by Mosby, and placed under guard. Eighty names were struck from our rolls that day, and started for Richmond under a guard of twenty-three men. Out of the eighty, only twenty-three were turned over to Major Boyle, Provost Marshal at Gordonsville. Some of them escaped by jumping out of a window in the third story of a house; others would leave their horses, &c. After inspection, the men were disbanded, to go to their homes and await further orders.

On the 16th of November, a meeting of Company D was held at Paris. Thirty men reported for duty, and started on a raid into the Valley, commanded by Captain Montjoy. They passed through Ashby's Gap at noon, and the Shenandoah River at the Island Ford one mile below Berry's Ferry. Montjoy then shaped his course in the direction of Winchester, avoiding on his march the public roads and highways. His movements in the Valley being entirely under cover of night, he succeeded in reaching the vicinity of Winchester without being observed by any one, either friend or foe. Concealing himself and men in a piece of woodland until day, and resting and feeding their horses at sunrise, he sallied out in quest of *game*.

It was not long before Montjoy, who was ahead some distance *prospecting*, came back and reported the enemy advancing in a force he intended to attack. He drew up his men for the charge under a hill about one hundred yards from the road leading from Winchester to Newtown. The enemy moved up slowly and carelessly, and little dreamed they were marching into the lion's jaws, or that a mere handful of *Johnnies* (one third their number) were lying a few rods from them, eager for the fray. When they were directly opposite his men, Montjoy ordered the charge. The enemy were struck on the flank and rear. So great was the suprise, and impetuous the charge, that little or no resistance was shown by them. They all, to a man, put spurs to their horses, to escape the best way they could. Twelve, however, bit the dust in the space of about one mile, and seventeen were captured, including the same number of horses.

On Montjoy's return to Fauquier, while passing through Berryville, he met Captain Brasher, alias Blazer, with about seventy-five men. The meeting was a surprise to both parties, and had Captain Montjoy, instead of inquiring who they were, charged through them, as Mosby would have done, Brasher would have been routed, and his men scattered over the whole Valley. But during the colloquy, time was afforded Brasher to form his men by one of his lieutenants (Cole), and thus get the *bulge* on Montjoy, which resulted in a precipitate retreat. Captain Montjoy and his men were pursued to the Shenandoah River, losing two men killed and five wounded, besides abandoning all his capture.

CHAPTER XXXIV

THE BRAVE BRASHER DEFEATED AND TAKEN PRISONER — MAGNA-
NIMITY OF BRAVE MEN — CAPTURES — CAPTURES RE-CAPTURED —
ESCAPE OF YOUNG ROLLING.

ON the 17th of November, the First Squadron, Companies A and B, met at Bloomfield, while the Second Squadron, Companies C, E, and F, met at Paris, and went into the Valley, capturing four horses and three prisoners near Winchester, and returned on the 18th. The First Squadron, commanded by Captain A. E. Richards, crossed the mountains at Snicker's Gap, and the Shenandoah River at Castleman's Ferry. From there Richards pushed on down the Valley to Cabletown, in search of Captain Brasher. Reaching Cabletown, Richards learned that Brasher had just gone in search of him, in the direction of Rock Ford. Getting on his track, Richards followed him up, and, when about midway between the Ford and Cabletown, met him in an open field.

Company B halted under a hill, while Company A was sent ahead, to pull down a fence. Brasher, thinking A retreating, charged them; but before reaching Company A, Richards, with Company B, charged them on their flank. A desperate fight ensued, a portion of which was hand-to-hand. The enemy broke and retreated in confusion, and were pursued for several miles. The field was strewn with their dead and wounded. Brasher, who fought as no Federal soldier ever fought before, after a hand-to-hand fight with Sidney Ferguson, who knocked him off his horse with a pistol, surrendered. Thirty-one of the enemy were killed and wounded; nineteen were taken prisoners, together with thirty-nine fine horses. Brasher, when he made the attack, had six prisoners with him, — three of General Lomax's men, and three of ours, whom they had captured the day before in the Valley. Puryear, one of them, as soon as he was liberated, picked up a club in one hand, and with a pistol which he had borrowed, in the other, went in, knocking down on one side and shooting on the other.

Richards had one man killed and six wounded. He had only seventy-five men with him, while Brasher had his whole command (one hundred men) with him. Brasher complimented Richards highly for his bravery and skill in the management of his men, saying he never saw men fight better, and that he had been whipped fairly, a compliment that affected Harry Hatcher so sensibly, that he could not refrain from embracing the old soldier, although he was a foe.

When the North heard of this complete overthrow of the man who had been taken from the regular army, and sent to the Valley with one hundred picked men, to "*clean out Mosby*," by one third fewer men than he had, and armed with nothing but pistols, their newspapers teemed with explanations, and insisted that the case was not so bad as was at first supposed. It might not have been so; but one thing is certain, Captain Brasher was so crippled in this engagement, that his men who escaped never made another raid into our Confederacy, or exchanged shots on the battle-field. When he was exchanged, the authorities gave a Confederate Colonel for this captain.

On the 20th of November, a meeting of the members of Company F was held at Paris. Lieutenant Frank Trurun, commanding, took twenty-five men, crossed the mountains and entered the Valley, and captured, near Summit Point, eight prisoners, and the same number of mules and horses. Sending them out with a guard of five men, he pushed on with the remaining twenty to the neighborhood of Winchester, and captured on the 22d fifteen prisoners and fifteen horses, and returned to Fauquier, on the 23d, without loss.

On the 21st, Companies C and D met at Paris, Montjoy commanding. Mosby took them into the Valley, and on the 22d, when near Winchester, captured nineteen prisoners and seventeen mules, which were brought out and sold to the Government.

On the 23d of November, Companies C and E met at Paris. Only sixty-five men reported for duty. At four o'clock P.M., led by Lieutenant John Russell, they passed through Ashby's Gap, and crossed the Shenandoah River at Berry's Ferry. Russell then moved in the direction of White Post. Here he hid his men in the woods, until Mosby and Captain William Chapman should come up.

They arrived at midnight, after a short rest. Lookouts were posted on all the roads, to watch for wagon-trains. Seeing nothing, they were called in, and Mosby moved his men nearer Winchester. While emerging from a piece of wood, they saw a train of wagons in the distance. Pushing up his men, Mosby charged the train, and followed it into General Powell's cavalry camp of two thousand men. The enemy fled in all directions, leaving Mosby to start out with one hundred and fifty prisoners and two hundred horses and mules. The enemy, however, rallied and pursued Mosby. Mosby's horse became unmanageable, broke his bit, and ran away. The men followed him, and were pushed so close as to necessitate an abandonment of all the prisoners and captured property.

In the retreat, Captain Chapman had his horse killed under him. John Kirwin, one of his men, dismounted from his Rosinante, and gave him to his captain, while he himself jumped up behind another man, and came out safe. Young Bolling had his horse shot, and fell with him, playing dead. The enemy came up, took one thousand two hundred dollars out of his pocket, and passed on.

After they had all disappeared, Bolling got up, shook himself, and started afoot to Fauquier. Angelo, alias Mocking-bird, was captured, and taken to Martinsburg and put in jail. During the first night of his incarceration, he opened the jail door, walked out, and escaped, reaching Fauquier the next day. These were all the casualties on this raid. The pursuit terminated at Millwood, five miles from the Shenandoah River.

CHAPTER XXXV.

DEATH OF MONTJOY—BURNING OF JOE BLACKWELL'S HOUSE, MOSBY'S HEADQUARTERS—A LOYAL TRANSACTION IN WOOL—RAID OF CUSTAR AND OTHERS—DESTRUCTION AND DESOLATION.

ON the 26th of this month, the First and Second Squadrons met at Bloomfield. Two hundred men reported for duty. Mosby, placing himself at the head of the column, moved off to Snickersville. Passing through the Gap and crossing the Shenandoah River, he pushed on to Charlestown, to attack a cavalry camp at that place. On reaching Charlestown, it was found that Captain Baylor, of the regular army, had attacked them the night before, and they had been reënforced with three hundred infantry posted in a church near by. Deeming it inexpedient to make an attack, Mosby abandoned the expedition, disbanded his men, and all returned. The Second Squadron met the same day at Paris, crossed over into the Valley, and captured only three horses and three Feds, and returned.

Montjoy, with Company D, went to Loudon County after Keyes, who had been raiding there with impunity. Entering Leesburg, Montjoy met and attacked him. Keyes made a precipitate retreat towards his rendezvous, the Point of Rocks, with Montjoy after him. Three miles from town, Montjoy, being far ahead of his men, was bushwhacked, and received a mortal wound in the head, just over the eye. He was carried to Leesburg by his men, and left in charge of kind and warm friends. Here he lingered only a few hours.

In the fall of Captain R. P. Montjoy, Mosby lost one of the most brilliant officers in his command, gallant and brave to a fault. A poor boy from Mississippi, he raised himself to the command of Company D by his own industry. Through his sobriety, skill, courage, and amiable manners, he enjoyed the esteem of his men and the confidence of his commander. Twenty-four horses and fifteen prisoners were brought away, the fail of Montjoy being the only casualty. Jim Chilton and Bob Crawford distinguished themselves in this engagement by their dashing conduct.

While we were absent this month on a raid, the enemy came up from Falls Church and burnt Joe Blackwell's house, Mosby's headquarters. Their treatment of Mr. Blackwell's family was of a most unsoldierly character. The family were turned out of doors, and not even permitted to take with them a change of clothing. Nothing was left on the plantation but the spring-house. They even applied the torch to the chicken-coops. In the destruction of this house, Colonel Mosby lost all his reports, correspondence, and other valuable papers pertaining to the command. After the destruction of Mr. Blackwell's house, Colonel Mosby established his headquarters at Holland's Factory, two miles and a half from Rectortown. This factory derived its name from the owner, Mr. Holland, a Union man. Attached to the factory was the private residence of Mr. Holland, who owned the factory.

While Holland was absent in Washington, the tolls from the carding of the wool were very heavy; and after a large quantity had accumulated on Mrs. Holland's hands, she would communicate the fact to Mr. Holland. He would then bring a large force of the enemy up to the factory, by whom the wool was carried out in the road and set on fire. The enemy leaving immediately, a stream of water was turned on it and the fire extinguished. Holland would return to Washington, file his claim, and get pay for his wool; and it is a notorious fact in Fauquier, he has told reliable citizens there, that he received pay from the Government for every pound burnt, and in some burnings treble the amount that he had on hand. Here Mosby held his headquarters until the surrender, and although the enemy made repeated visits to this factory, they never disturbed anything.

On the 28th of November, a dense fog hung over Fauquier all day: so thick was it that objects could not be distinguished a distance of ten yards. The enemy, availing themselves of it, crossed the Shenandoah River at Berry's Ferry with three divisions (about eight thousand cavalry), and made that celebrated raid through Fauquier and Loudon Counties, in which they burnt every barn, stable, wheat, hay, and straw-rick, and mill, and everything that man or beast could subsist upon, and all the stock, cattle, &c., they could see were driven off. The divisions consisted of Custar's, Torbert's, and Merritt's. Commencing at Peter Hartman's, Mrs. Edmonds', and William Hopper's, they burnt every mill, — including the celebrated Reed Mill, whose flour took the premium at the World's Fair in London, — barn, stable, hay and straw-rick and wheat-stack, and even shocks of corn in the field; every cow, horse, sheep, and hog they could see was driven off, not a single thing being left for the people to subsist upon except a little the people had hid in the mountains, for an emergency. When hogs had been killed by the farmers and hung up to cool off, these men would take an axe, chop the hams off, and drop the remainder in the mud. One mile from Upperville, where they camped the first night, a widow lady, Mrs. Fletcher, was having a load of hogs brought home from a neighbor's to salt. When the wagon crossed the turnpike going to Mrs. Fletcher's, the enemy took her oxen to their camp and burnt up the wagon with the pork. This was all the meat that poor widow had to feed her children with the ensuing summer.

The next day they established their headquarters at Snickersville, and remained there for three days, and during that time applied the torch to everything except the houses: these they robbed. In some portions of Loudon, Quakers and Union citizens were spared; but along under the mountains, from Semper's Mill to Leesburg, none escaped the fury of the enemy. The poor people, with only one cow for their subsistence, were deprived of it. If old Satan himself had thrown open the gates of hell, and turned loose all the devils in there, they could not have inflicted greater misery and woe than Custar's, Torbert's, and Merritt's cavalry inflicted on these people in this raid. To see that they did their work of destruction thoroughly, General Custar himself, the second day after he crossed at Berry's Ferry, with a large force scoured the Blue Ridge Mountains from Snickersville to Ashby's Gap. On entering Paris, and halting with his body-guard in front of Mr. Adams's, keeper of the hotel, he ordered his men "to get to work and complete the destruction of everything that might be of service to Mosby," and to show his men no quarter. Two of his body-guard went to Mr. Hartman, to get their *rations*. While one was in the milk-house, doing his dirty work,

Sid Ferguson rode up and seized him by the collar and carried him off. General Custar, fearing he might meet with the same fate, made a hasty retreat to Mrs. Hicks's, two miles down the turnpike, where he rejoined a portion of his men, who had swept everything before them.

How agreeable must have been General Custar's reflections, as he viewed from the top of the Blue Ridge, immense clouds of smoke and flame, arising from smouldering ruins, as far as the eye could reach, — the ruins of the houses of a once happy and prosperous people, now reduced to absolute beggary by his hand and edict. Recollections of that character may be drowned in the excitement of active life and the storm of the battle-field, but on the death-bed they will rise up as they appeared to him on the 29th day of November, 1864.

About fifty of the burners were captured and shot. One was taken to Mount Eddy, and with his eyes looking down on the smoking ruins wrought by his own hands, was hung. At Mrs. Burns's, near Upperville, they caught John Thomas, of Company A, and beat him, as they thought, to death. He, however, "played possum," and, after they left, got up, minus his pistols and pocket-book. Fully realizing his situation, John took a position on the roadside, and waited for something to turn up. While he was reflecting on the vicissitudes of a partisan ranger's life, a straggler came along. Thomas seized the reins of the horse with one hand, and with the other hand dismounted his adversary before he had time to draw his pistols. Securing them, and mounting the fellow's horse, he escaped to the mountains just as the rear-guard was coming in sight.

WILLIAM R. SMITH

CHAPTER XXXVI.

INTENSE COLD INTERFERES WITH OPERATIONS — MOSBY SEVERELY WOUNDED — DILIGENT SEARCH FOR HIM — THE NEST WARM, BUT THE BIRD FLOWN — PROMOTIONS — "FEAST OF REASON," ETC. — MAJOR RICHARDS "PROCURES SUPPLIES."

ON the 2d of December, Mosby started to Richmond, to make arrangements for forage for his men's horses for the next campaign, and lay the matter of this burning before the President.

On the 3d of December, a meeting of the whole battalion was held at Upperville. The First squadron went into the Valley, crossing at Snicker's Gap and Castleman's Ferry. Proceeding then to Charlestown, and finding no enemy, Captain A. E. Richards pushed on to the Baltimore and Ohio Railroad at Duffield Station, placing obstructions on the track, to capture a train of cars. After waiting patiently all night for one to approach, and none making its appearance, the men were disbanded, and all returned to Fauquier.

The Second squadron, commanded by Captain William H. Chapman, crossed over into the Valley at Berry's Ferry, and when near the White Post, were attacked by an overwhelming force of the enemy, which necessitated their retreat. That was effected without loss or injury.

On the 7th of December another inspection of the command was held at Rectortown. Captain Clary, of General Early's staff, was the inspecting officer; but no further *details* were made to the regular army. After inspection, Captain Richards, of Company B, and commandant of the First squadron, detailed forty men, with fast horses, to meet him the next day (Thursday), at two o'clock, at Snickersville.

In compliance with Richards's order, the men met him. He then started on a raid to the Valley, crossing the mountains at Snicker's Gap, and Shenandoah River at Castleman's Ferry. Penetrating the enemy's lines to within five miles of Martinsburg, and capturing only two Federals, he changed his course, and struck for the Baltimore and Ohio Railroad, near Duffield Station. When about half way a violent snow-storm set in and compelled him to return to Fauquier. As it snowed all that night, Richards's men suffered severely. He reached headquarters, however, without loss or serious injury, although the mercury stood below zero during his entire absence.

On the 10th of December, Captain Sam Chapman, commanding Company E, took thirty of his men into the Valley, crossing at Ashby's Gap, and the river at Island Forde, in a terrible snow-storm. He bivouacked that night on the banks of the Shenandoah, and at four o'clock the next morning mounted his men and attacked a picket post at the toll-gate, near Millwood, before day, with great success, capturing five Federals and eleven horses, without loss.

On the night of the 21st of December, Colonel Mosby, with only one man (Love), was surprised and wounded. He fell into the hands of the *Philistines* at Mr. Lake's, near Rector's Cross Roads. Colonel Mosby, with young Love, was returning from a scouting expedition in one of the lower counties, and, feeling very much fatigued, they stopped in at Mr. Lake's, at nine o'clock at night, to refresh themselves with a cup of genuine coffee.

Believing no enemy to be nearer than Middleburg, he went into the house. However, to guard against any accident or surprise, he put Love on picket, to watch the road leading to the Cross Roads. He had been in the house but a few minutes, when a party of one hundred of the Eighth Illinois cavalry came up the Salem road and captured Love before he could give any alarm by firing his pistol. Mosby, hearing an unusual noise, like the rattling of sabres, in the road, jumped up from the table and went to the door to see what was the matter. On his opening the front door, a large squad was waiting for him, who instantly demanded his surrender. Closing that door, he retreated to the back door, but found no avenue of escape through it, as a large squad were there. He then concluded, as a last resort, to try one of the front windows, thinking that by jumping through it into the darkness amongst them, he might, in the confusion, escape unobserved. Divesting himself of his elegant military coat and jacket, with no insignia of rank on, or of his being a Confederate soldier, except a pair of gray pantaloons, he approached the window, when he was fired upon from the road, and fell, dangerously wounded.

The Miss Lakes, fearing Mosby's rank would betray him, took his jacket (which had two stars on the collar), and hid it under a lounge. The enemy, as soon as Mosby fell, rushed into the house to see what officer it was they had shot, through the window. They were met at the door by Miss Lake, who told them "*That man you shot is dying!*" Several of them went into the room where he was stretched out on the floor, in the throes of death. He could yet speak a little. On being asked what his name was, and where shot, he told them he was "*Lieutenant Johnson, of the Third Virginia cavalry.*" His speech failing him at that moment, and the enemy imagining he was really dying, relieved him of his boots, military cloak, pocketbook, and papers, and left him. Love, who was a prisoner in the road, had all this time kept silent as to who the officer was in the house. In the meanwhile, some of the party who were in the house, rejoined the column in the road, and related what had transpired. Love, overhearing the conversation, and feeling the greatest anxiety for the safety of his colonel, and seeing they did not know who it was, "took the cue," and determined not to tell them, and thus afford Mr. Lake an opportunity (if Mosby was not too dangerously wounded,) to carry him to a safe place.

Love was carried to Middleburg. On the road he was interrogated as to who that officer was in the house. He replied that he was a stranger to him, but he *understood* his name to be Lieutenant Johnson, of the Regular Service. The enemy, satisfied it was not their great terror (Mosby), troubled themselves no further about him until they reached their camp, when on examining the papers in the pockets of the clothes they had taken from Lieutenant Johnson, to their utter amazement, they found it was no other person than the veritable John S. Mosby, and not Lieutenant Johnson! The greatest excitement prevailed in and through the camp. The command " to horse," was instantly given by the officer in command, and the whole force started back to Mr. Lake's, to secure Lieutenant Johnson, and bring him to camp, dead or alive.

The return was a most exciting march. Men vied with their officers to reach Mr. Lake's first. Mr. Lake, however, who was a great admirer and warm personal friend of

Colonel Mosby, had not been unmindful of the Colonel's critical situation, and what a serious loss his capture would be to the people of Fauquier, and the Confederacy. Without considering the treatment he would receive at their hands, Mr. Lake, as soon as the enemy left the house, yoked up his steers, and placed him in an *ox-cart*, in an almost dying condition, and drove him through the fields, (to prevent the enemy's getting on his track) to Mr. Quilly Glasscock's, father of Lieutenant Glasscock, a mile and a half distant on Goose Creek, and off the public road. Ere Mosby had reached Mr. Glasscock's, the enemy were back to Mr. Lake's for their prize; but the bird had flown. The house was searched diligently, but no one found. They raved. The ladies of the house were taken out and interrogated as to where that wounded man was, and told that if they did not tell, their house should be burned down. The only reply they received was, "Burn on, we do not know where he is."

The enemy, satisfying themselves he was not on Mr. Lake's premises, and not knowing at what moment they might be attacked at that hour of the night, fell into line and moved back to their camp, with the intention of renewing the search the next morning.

At Mr. Glasscock's, Dr. Dunn, surgeon of the battalion, and Dr. Eliason, late of General Stuart's Staff, were soon at his side. His wound was pronounced dangerous and painful, being through the side, just below the ribs, producing internal bleeding, so that he was not in a condition to be moved. Yet he was kept in an ambulance, with fleet horses harnessed up, ready to be moved in an emergency.

The enemy returned next day, and after a fruitless search returned that evening to Fairfax. Doctors Dunn and Eliason pronouncing Mosby's wounds too dangerous to admit of his being moved, the men were employed in picketing all the roads, to give notice of the approach of the enemy. For fear the enemy might find out Mosby's whereabouts, he was moved in the night from one neighbor's house to another, by which means they were not only ignorant of where he was, but even his own men did not know. His men, however, knew he was in the neighborhood, and that was all.

The Monday night after he was shot, he

was carried to Salem. Tuesday morning five thousand Federal cavalry arrived in Salem, on their return to the Valley from a raid through Rappahannock and Madison Counties, to Gordonsville. They had heard of Mosby's being wounded, and were looking out for him, knowing his friends would endeavor to get him inside of our lines, or to his father's in Amherst County. In Salem all inquired where he was, and large rewards were offered for the information. "*No one knows*" was all they could get out of the citizens of Salem; yet Mosby was amongst them at that moment. The enemy, dividing their force there into two columns, instituted a rigid search for the "guerilla." One column moved in the direction of Middleburg, destroying and burning everything in their route, except private residences. The other column moved through Rectortown and Piedmont, and camped on Joe Gibson's farm, two miles from Paris, that night. Generals Custar and Torbert establishing their headquarters in the mill, the roads and lanes were barricaded, to keep us from disturbing them.

Lieutenants Beattie and John Russell, with some few men, annoyed the enemy all night.

Sky-rockets were thrown into their camp, and the cattle and stock they had stolen from the citizens along their route were frightened and stampeded. Their camp being between two mountains, and our men being on the sides, they amused themselves by throwing hand-grenades in amongst them, rolling large rocks down on them, and firing into them. Their situation, and the sleep they had that night, can be better imagined by my readers than I relate to them. The enemy visited Jim Lew Adams, and charged him with having boarded and given aid, comfort, and sympathy to our men. According to Judge Lynch (under whose code they decided such cases), accusation and conviction being synonymous terms, they destroyed every article upon which his family might subsist, including bedding, clothing, corn, and poultry, carrying off such articles as suited their fancy. They likewise made a call upon Mr. William Hopper, near the Gap. Mrs. Hopper had anticipated the object of their mission, and secreted the contents of the smoke-house under the wood-pile. Just as her undertaking was completed, the squad came into the yard and ordered refreshments, which were not furnished according to a regular bill of fare, when they broke into the smoke-house and feloniously captured two rolls of sausage. At Mrs. Margaret Edmonds's, they discovered some good bacon in the garret, which was hastily confiscated. The sanctity of her private chamber was broken, and the men acted without restraint. From thence they crossed the mountains at Ashby's Gap, in the direction of Winchester. In the Gap, there lived at the house of Peter Marshall, a faithful old black woman, who, for the love she bore her *true* friends, had received and given shelter to our pickets on divers occasions. By some means not known to the writer, the Yankees had learned of this old woman's fidelity, and forthwith she was robbed of all her food and little " traps."

Captain Richards and Bob Walker, with fifteen Virginia boys, followed close in the wake of these plunderers as they crossed the river, and even to the vicinity of Millwood, from whence our men retraced their steps, encountering a dense fog, under cover of which the remaining division of the Yankee forces came upon our men unawares. Our men were very "impressionable" at this juncture of affairs, and effected their escape with some rapidity and considerable eclat, by taking to the mountains.

It was on the day of these occurrences that several promotions were made in the command, for gallant services, and meritorious conduct, Mosby receiving a Colonel's commission, Captain William H. Chapman, that of Lieutenant-Colonel, and Captain A. E. Richards, that of Major.

December 29th, was the day on which another search was inaugurated for Mosby. Some three hundred men of the Eighth Illinois Cavalry came from Fairfax, and worked with great industry in their hunt. Mosby was hard by, and on two occasions was completely in their power, if they had known it. Some of the prisoners captured were at a loss to account for Mosby's ubiquitous character, charged our men with making underground railroads, and acting a la Mosby above ground, while the original Mosby escaped through some subterranean passage.

The last forty-eight hours of the old year brought us violent snow-storms, gloomy and freezing-cold rains, hail and sleet, and consequently not much activity was displayed.

The Second Squadron, consisting of Companies C, E, F, and G, met at Salem on the 3d day of January, 1864, and made preparations to take up winter quarters on the Northern Neck, comprising the Counties of King George, Westmoreland, Northumberland, Lancaster, and Richmond, lying between the Rappahannock and Potomac rivers, a section of country not having been occupied or visited by the forces of either side, and one of the richest portions of the Old Dominion. Forage and commissary stores existed in abundance, and food was a desideratum, as the Yankees had swept the country around the Neck, with a sort of patent broom, which deprived men and non-combatants alike, of the necessaries of life. Our preparations, however, were completed, when it was whispered that the Graces desired to honor us with an entertainment, and friendly reception. A *dejeuner* was prepared under the auspices of the beautiful Virginia girls, Misses Cochrane, Murray, Welch, and their lovely associates, which did honor to the donors and the occasion. We were served with dressed turkey, roast pork, beef *a la mode*, cake, hot coffee, etc. Notwithstanding these savory viands met a cordial welcome with the physical man, the nobler impulses of our soul were gently touched with admiration and emotions akin to love for the accomplishments and unostentatious hospitality of our fair friends. It was, moreover, a feast of reason, beauty, grace, and refinement, and an interchange of wishes, hopes, and prayers for the success of our sacred cause.

During the *tête a tête*, and amidst the fugue of voices which rung in every tone, semi-tone and key, falling in sweet cadence, and enriched ever and anon by bursts of sparkling wit and pathos, one of our boys brought the house to breathless silence. In a stentorian voice the question was asked: "Why are Virginians engaged in war?" Immediately Miss —— arose, and extemporaneously alluded to the cause of the war with a modest diction which nerved every fibre of our souls with the sentiment, that,

"Thrice is he armed who hath his quarrel just."

She said in substance:

"Soldiers! Liberty is your watchword. Causes which are not ephemeral have led you to seek the establishment of an independent Government, organized with such powers as may be derived from the consent of the governed. You have never denied to others the rich boon you seek. Aggression, and open declarations, and overt acts of hostility to our wronged and injured people, have impelled you to defend your altars and homes. Our enemies know the honesty and justice of the struggle, but systematically falsify history. Recur, if you please, to the published crusade contained in the infamous Helper Book, the teaching of the Stowes, Beechers, Dickinsons, Phillipses, Greeleys, and abolition conclaves, the Nat Turner Insurrections, John Brown raid, Kansas Border wars, Lincoln's dictum that the *Government cannot endure permanently, half slave and half free*,—the organization of Manufacturers' Leagues in the North, forcing us to pay tribute by exorbitant tariffs, accompanied by their "*Wide Awake*" mobs and Personal Liberty-Free-Negro-Bills, the declaration of an Irrepressible Conflict, the dogma of Federal consolidation and infringement of reserved, vested rights. These are some of the causes which inspire and move you. The instinct which drives the worm to turn under the tread, is engrafted in your natures; hence you resist coercion and subjugation by the natural laws of self-defence. Nay, you fight to perpetuate and hand down to posterity, the patriotic principles enunciated by our Washington, Jefferson, Monroe, Madison, Marshall and Henry."

Company D travelled from Hooper's shop, on the turnpike near Middleburg, to the vicinity of Fairfax, touching at Centreville, thence to Gainesville. Night, darkness and foul weather were wholly disregarded. The command, being in charge of Major Richards, were occasionally divided into squads, one of which, led by Captain Glasscock, attacked a train on the Orange and Alexandria Railroad, near Alexandria, without material success, more than to remind our enemies that we had not " froze out."

Major Richards resolved to strike a blow which should be felt by the sentimental, infallible gentry, and accordingly ordered eighty men to concentrate at Bloomfield. From hence they hastened across the mountains, via Snicker's Gap, fording the river at Castleman's Ferry, passing through Cabletown and Charlestown, and called a halt at Duffield Station, on the Baltimore and Ohio Railroad.

Simultaneous with their arrival, a richly laden freight train hove in sight. Upon an exchange of cards, the train was confiscated. A vote of thanks was extended to the provident Yankee Quartermaster, for our supplies of coffee, sugar, clothing, crackers, fish, &c. Indeed, the success inspired the men with delight to such a degree that the visit was prolonged for several hours, trusting that the express train would run into their tender embrace. An alarm was sounded, but before the command had fully retired, the Express train came thundering forward, like a shooting star, and was suddenly brought to a complete smash-up by the debris of the freight train. This was a casualty of war, and the curses heaped upon Mosby were neither select nor elegant. The Union-savers soon repaired the damage and arrested sundry non-combatants, to surfeit their revenge.

CHAPTER XXXVII.

EXPLOIT OF MAJOR RICHARDS — RUMORS OF PEACE NEGOTIATIONS — DEEP SNOW — FOX-HUNTING — MAJOR GIBSON AND LIEUTENANT BAKER AFTER US — SOME OF THEM RETURN — NOBLE CONDUCT OF LIEUTENANT BAKER.

THE dawn of the morning of February 1, 1865, was heralded by still another exploit of Major Richards with twenty-five men. They made another crossing at Castleman's, and captured five patrolmen, from whom, by the exercise of strength, awkwardness, and a mixture of deception, they succeded in obtaining the countersign, and thus armed were enabled to effect the loan of five noble chargers from the Yankee garrison at Charlestown. The conditions of the loan not being fully understood, several leaden messengers sung around their ears as they made their exit. The riders of the captured horses were induced to remain in the saddle until we could furnish them quarters. Upon the return of Major Richards, he was advised that Jim

Wilcher and Bob Eastham, (alias Bob Ridley), with ten men, had attacked a train between Harper's Ferry and Winchester, without success. The engineer, however, fell from the train in his frenzied efforts to save his charge, and was instantly killed.

About this time rumors were in circulation of peace negotiations, and a conference to that end was said to be on the tapis at Fortress Monroe, between Vice President Stephens, Hon. Mr. Hunter, and Campbell, and Messrs. Lincoln and Seward. The news was brought by Bush Underwood, who had been scouting in Fairfax with four men. The intelligence cast a gloom not only over the officers and men, but over the whole of Mosby's "Confederacy;" and, although the farmers and soldiers were living on half allowance, gold at one hundred, and the citizens refusing to take Confederate money, we did not relax our efforts in the least degree. The officers and men unanimously resolved that if the Confederacy went down, the present generation and those that came after them should not say we did not discharge our duty. The men began to accumulate forage for their horses for the approaching campaign. They commenced collecting the tithe in Fauquier, but that was discontinued, by order of Colonel Mosby, in consequence of the heavy tax which the people had already paid, in boarding his men.

On the 6th of February, Major Richards started with five men on a scouting expedition to Fairfax; but was obliged, before he got half way, to return, in consequence of a violent snow-storm which set in. The snow fell to the depth of two feet, and in many places where it drifted, it was one hundred feet. Roads were blockaded with it, and the stock in the mountains died for the want of grazing. While this condition of the roads lasted, the men amused themselves with the exciting sport of fox-chasing. Day and night could be heard the barking of dogs and the music of the horn reverberating in the mountains. A grand chase was proposed by some of the old hunters, and it came off on the 8th of February. The snow was about eighteen inches deep. Hunters came from the adjoining counties with their dogs. The foxes had become very annoying to the farmers in this portion of Fauquier, and as all kinds of business and work were suspended, it was thought an excellent time to terminate the career of some of them. The old hunters, Wm. Hopper, Reuben Triplett, Bob and Phil Eastham, Hand, and John Carr had the management of it. One hundred citizens and soldiers participated in the chase. There were one hundred hounds, and the reverberations of their barking through the mountains, combined with the sight of a hundred men engaged in the chase, was a thing long to be remembered by the people of Fauquier. In dashing over the ravines men would sometimes be precipitated into the banks of snow, but soon recovered themselves. The chase commenced at ten o'clock A.M., and terminated at sunset. Five foxes were caught, and a large number chased to their caves.

On the 18th of February, one hundred and twenty-five of the Fourteenth Pennsylvania Cavalry, commanded by Major Gibson and Lieutenant Baker, of General Merritt's staff, crossed the Shenandoah River at Shepherd's Mill, nine miles from Paris, at eleven o'clock P.M., and made a night raid into our Confederacy, confident that we had abandoned our huts and holes in the mountains during this severe weather, and were sleeping in the farmers' houses again. The weather was, and had been for some time, intensely cold. Snow was deep on the ground, and they were sure of making "*a good thing of it.*" After crossing at Shepherd's Mill, they took the road under the mountains and struck the turnpike at Mount Carmel Church. Here they were joined by another party of two hundred, who had crossed at Berry's Ferry. Passing through the Gap, they reached Paris at the foot of the mountain. Here they separated. The party of two hundred, which crossed at Berry's Ferry, were to proceed down the turnpike to Upperville, and capture Major Richards at his father's, two miles beyond, at Green Garden Mills; thence to Rectortown and Piedmont, where they were to meet the other party, after searching every house in their route. The other party, Major Gibson's, was to take the mountain road to Markham, and from there proceed to Piedmont.

The first party, after searching every house on the turnpike, entered Upperville. There they found a Government agent, with five barrels of apple-brandy, which he had brought up to Fauquier to trade with the farmers for hospital supplies. This was confiscated. The heads of the barrels were knocked out, and all hands got drunk. By the time they reached Major Richards, they were too drunk to effect anything. They, however, surrounded the house. A party knocked at the front door, and were admitted by the Major's father. Taking him at first for the Major, they subjected him to a little rough treatment, until, by showing them his locks, frosted by many winters, he induced them to release him. The Major, who heard them before they entered the house, secreted himself in a place in the wall, which he had specially prepared for this exigency. The house and premises were searched diligently; but the object of their visit was not to be found. However, they appropriated to themselves every stitch of clothing he had in the world, including a magnificent dress uniform and overcoat, which he had received but a few days before from Baltimore. Being too drunk to proceed any further, this party returned to the Valley before day.

Major Gibson performed his part like a soldier, searching every house diligently on his route, except Mr. Hopper's and Mr. Hartman's at the foot of the Gap. How they overlooked them I am unable to comprehend. Had they given Mr. Hopper a call, five would have been caught sleeping in a feather bed, including the writer. Soldiers, however, you know, are inclined to be superstitious. They remembered the last 18th of February, and that their friends were languishing in Northern prisons from the treachery of one of their own countrymen. Some of the old members had become careless, and returned to their feather-beds. Those that returned, and new ones, were all captured. While at Mrs. Betsy Edmonds', Clem Edmonds, George Triplett, and Sam Alexander, heard them from their *ranch* in the mountains, about half a mile in rear of the house. Saddling their horses, and convincing themselves who they were, they started out and gave the alarm. Proceeding ahead to Lieutenant Wren's, who was staying at Mr. Brown's, about one mile distant, they were joined by him and a few others, and followed the enemy up to Piedmont. Reaching this place at daylight, Gibson expected to find the other column. Not hearing anything from them at sunrise, he started back to the Valley, taking the turnpike to Upperville, and thence up to Paris,

Lieutenant Wren following him, but not doing anything except keeping them closed up. Every chicken and turkey-roost in their route had been robbed by them, and each man had his turkey or old hen strapped behind his saddle, together with the clothing, &c., which they had taken from the citizens. At Mr. Chapplier's, two miles from Piedmont, on the turnpike to Upperville, J. Wright James, our Quartermaster, was captured. By this time their presence in our midst became generally known amongst our men; who displaying themselves on the hills and mountains, the enemy became alarmed, and pushed on rapidly from Mr. Chapplier's to Upperville. Not finding any of our men there except Grafton Carlisle, they pushed on rapidly up the turnpike, and reached Paris about nine o'clock A.M.

Major Richards, in the meanwhile, heard of this party, and having no clothes of his own, he put on a suit of his father's brown jeans, mounted his horse, and started after them. At Upperville he met with Lieutenant Wren, with a few men. Pushing on up the turnpike, at Paris he was joined by others, who swelled his party to *thirty-eight men*. In

Paris some skirmishing took place between the enemy's rear-guard and Richards. The enemy retreated rapidly though the Gap, and formed on the other side of the mountain, at Mount Carmel Church, two miles from Paris.

The pursuit of Richards was conducted without any order whatever. His thirty-eight men were strung out for one quarter of a mile. But on dashed the gallant Richards. At the foot of Mt. Carmel he ordered the charge. The enemy, seeing with what resolution the charge was made, and imagining five thousand guerillas were after them, broke and retreated by the road they came. It was a narrow defile through the mountains, just large enough for one wagon to pass. Through this defile or road they had to retreat seven miles, where they were to cross the Shenandoah River by a dangerous ford, before they could entertain any idea of being safe. When they broke and got into this road, Richards' men closed in on them, and the slaughter was terrible. Along this road, clean down to the river, were strewn the dead, wounded, and prisoners. It was indeed a sickening sight. The snow this entire distance was crimson with the blood of the dead and wounded.

Every man of ours they had captured (twenty-five) was re-taken, besides one hundred mules and horses they had taken from the citizens (which were returned to them by Richards). Ten or fifteen were killed, eighty odd were captured and wounded, and brought to Paris. Major Gibson was wounded, captured, brought to Paris, and paroled with nine other badly wounded men.

Amongst the prisoners was Lieutenant Baker, of General Merrit's staff. When he was asked how he happened to be absent from his general, he stated that he had been on one or two of the night " excursions" in the Valley, had found them quite exciting and pleasant, and as his friend, Major Gibson, was going on this one, he concluded he would accompany him, and render his assistance in " arresting" us. But he counted the chickens before they were hatched. Their raid as far as Upperville was a decided success. And here their hopes failed them. They knew not at what moment they would be attacked by a set of *wolves*. Surrounded by these circumstances, very few men would fight with an enemy they did not understand. The men that were able to walk were sent to Richmond. Lieutenant Baker was furnished with a horse, by one of the men, to ride to Culpepper, where they took the cars for Richmond.

Major Richards, in this affair, had one man (John Iden) killed, already a wounded soldier, and one (Dr. Sowers, of Clark's County,) wounded. The enemy captured John Iden at his brother Tom's, and took a watch, a family piece, from John. As they were carrying him off prisoner, his aged mother, hearing of the captors' having taken the watch, went to Lieutenant Baker, stated her case, and he promptly had it returned to her. The enemy, rather chagrined at the conduct of Baker, after they got him away from the house, on the public highway, robbed him of everything. The writer was detailed by Major Richards to take charge of the prisoners and guard. In due course of time we reached Culpepper Court House, on the Orange and Alexandria Railroad. From there they were sent by rail to Gordonsville, and were that night turned over to Major Boyle, Provost Marshal of the Army of Northern Virginia.

The next morning, while in Major Boyle's

office, awaiting the arrival of the cars, he handed me a lock of hair, which he said Baker had taken from one of the prisoners, who had taken it from the young man that was killed, and asked that it might be returned to his mother. Such an act of feeling was so uncommon in the Yankee army, I have deemed it worthy of notice here. Feeling a curiosity to know who the person was, I inquired of Major Boyle, who told me he was an Englishman, and the lieutenant I brought out.

I expressed to Major Boyle a desire to visit Richmond, and he placed the prisoners in my charge. The train coming up in a few minutes, after a short stoppage we were soon on our way to the capital. Reaching Richmond at seven o'clock P.M., we marched down Main Street to the Libby Prison, and turned over our prisoners to Major Turner.

CHAPTER XXXVIII.

HIGH PRICES — FORAGING — SHERIDAN'S MARCH — MOSBY PREVENTED FROM FOLLOWING BY SWOLLEN STREAMS — EXPLOITS OF CAPTAIN GLASSCOCK AND LIEUTENANT THOMPSON — A CHALLENGE NOT ACCEPTED — DESTRUCTION OF DISTILLERIES.

AT that time, in Richmond, it was melancholy to contemplate the condition of affairs. Hemmed in on three sides by the enemy, their supplies cut off, and only one avenue over which they could escape or draw supplies; and that portion, the Virginia Central Road already exhausted, there seemed to be nothing in prospect but starvation. Bacon was twelve and fifteen dollars a pound; flour twelve hundred dollars a barrel; sugar fifteen dollars a pound; oysters five dollars a dozen; eggs one dollar apiece; corn seventy-five dollars a bushel; and board at the Spottswood, fifty dollars a day. Considering these prices rather extravagant for a private soldier, who was getting only fifteen dollars a month, I remained in Richmond only two days. Taking the cars to Gordonsville, I there met Colonel Mosby, on his way to rejoin his command. Mounting my horse, and swimming the Rapidan, night found me at Jack's shop. At daybreak the next morning I was wending my way through Madison Court House, thence through Washington, Rappahannock County, and reached Fauquier the day after the Colonel.

The day on which Colonel Mosby rejoined it, the command was ordered to proceed immediately to Loudon County, to collect forage for the ensuing campaign. The citizens were very kind to us, especially the Quakers. Mr. Elijah Holmes, the head of their church in that county, entertained eight or ten of us every night for a month, without charge. Mrs. Hoge and her accomplished daughters (another strong Union family) likewise contributed all in their power to make our stay amongst them as pleasant as possible. In Waterford, the stronghold of Unionism, every attention imaginable was shown us. In Leesburg, the people, especially the ladies, rejoiced to see their Southern friends once more. Private entertainments were given to us, and all was mirth for several days. Our men, notwithstanding these attentions, were collecting their tithes, and sending it back to our little Confederacy, all anticipating a prosperous and active campaign.

Early in this month Sheridan commenced his march up the Valley, to join Grant, then lying around Petersburg and Richmond. The people are familiar with the misery and woe he brought upon the people along the line of his march. Mosby had anticipated this movement, and ordered his men to meet him in Markem. The elements, however, prevailed against him. The spring rains had set in, and the water-courses were so swollen as to prevent their passage. Had it been otherwise, many of Sheridan's cavalry would have "gone up" on their march from Charlottesville to Tyre River, on the Lynchburg Railroad. Mosby, learning the condition of the water-courses, ordered us back to Loudon.

On the 12th of March, Mosby ordered fifty men to meet him at Leesburg. Twenty-five of them were sent to Fairfax, under Captain Glasscock; the other twenty-five, under Lieutenant Ed Thompson, were sent to Munson's Hill, near Washington City. Thompson captured a patrol of ten men and horses. Captain Glasscock, hearing of a scouting party of thirty of the Sixteenth New York Cavalry near the Court House, prepared to engage them, and, if possible, capture the whole party. Learning the road they were on, he divided his men, one half being under Lieutenant Briscoe, the others under himself. Concealing themselves in the woods until the enemy should pass, as soon as the rear-guard went by Briscoe, he charged them, while Glasscock charged them in front. The enemy fought gallantly, and in their efforts to cut their way through all were killed except three, who escaped, and a few who surrendered. Glasscock brought off eighteen horses, without sustaining any loss.

On the 18th of this month (March), Lieutenant Ed Thompson was ordered by Mosby to take a squad of men and visit Occaquan. Selecting fifteen tried men, he visited that historic ground, and captured fifteen cavalrymen, with their horses, without loss on his side.

On the 20th of March, our gallant men were advised that an expedition of five hundred Yankee cavalry and one thousand infantry had been dispatched from Harper's Ferry, for the purpose of driving us from our native heath. They marched out to Hillsboro, with songs of mirth and self-admiration ringing through hill and dale. The ground over which they marched had been rendered classic by marches, counter-marches, skirmishes, and repeated engagements. Many noble spirits had already been buried in this soil, and the little mounds here and there were but so many memorials or guide-posts, reminding the living soldier of the sacredness of his struggle for liberty.

The 21st of March, as the dawn illumined the eastern horizon, we were summoned by our gallant leader to assemble at Hamilton. The clarion notes of the bugle rallied one hundred and twenty-eight as noble hearts as ever beat in the bosom of man. Hamilton was the point at which the Yankees expected to make their grand *coup de main*. The Southern boys were posted, and ordered to lie in hugger-mugger near Quaker Church, whilst Captain Glasscock, with a scout of four or five picked men, should ascertain the designs of the invaders. The Yankees reached Hamilton about noon, and moved down the road toward our position without delay. Colonel Mosby arrived on the field, and after a brief consultation prepared to meet the invaders, and to, —

> "Strike for the green graves of our sires,
> God, and our native Land."

Fifty Yankees were sent out to meet us as decoys; and their charge upon our rear and left flank struck us like a young hurricane, and then rebounded. Their blow was not irresistible, neither were our men immovable, but their retreat was as sudden and precipitous as their charge. Mosby, Glasscock, and Bob Eastham, promptly rallied the men, and determined to return the compliment. The retreat was closely followed up until within half a mile of Hamilton, where the Yankees were posted in full force, and in all the splendor and pomp of martial array. There was no halting or hesitation, and our men went in to the feast set before them. As we neared them, an exchange of volleys took place, and before our sabres could reach their front rank it gave way, and so confused those in the rear, that they at once sought safety in the houses and sheds of Hamilton.

This was rather to our wish, as we were fully equal to the task of taking any single house. Colonel Mosby, however, called the men forth and formed them in an open field near the town. This movement was mistaken for a retreat; but Mosby, after the men were marshalled into line, waved his hat and shouted for the Yankees to advance. They came from their hiding-places, but seemed unwilling to meet us. We cannot apologize for their hesitancy in accepting the challenge but upon the conjecture that our handful of men must have been mistaken for the advance guard of a large force. A spirited exchange of shots was kept up until late in the evening, when the Yankees drew off and passed through Hamilton, and admitted in their exit that they had lost fifty-two killed, wounded, and missing. Their men who were taken prisoners acknowledged a defeat, with a loss of two captains killed. Among our boys, James Keith and Binford were killed at the head of the column. Captain Manning, John Chew, and Ben Fletcher, wounded. Among those complimented by Colonel Mosby for distinguished prowess, were Corbin and John Hipkins, the Colonel himself having one horse killed under him during the engagement. We lost, also, two of our men captured, who, no doubt, have met the sad fate of many others, under the convenient pretext of being guerillas.

That night we bivouacked near Hamilton, and at dawn of day next morning discovered that the condition of the roads and fair weather had induced the invaders to make an advance on Snickersville, Bloomfield, and Middleburg. Mosby determined to follow, and in doing so resorted to a series of stratagems and devices to draw the enemy into another engagement. Their infantry, however, formed and marched in hollow squares, with the cavalry in the inclosure. This novel mode of protecting gay cavaliers did honor to the infantry, but the cavalry must have left their "*grit*" at the Ferry. We continued the pursuit below Middleburg, where the enemy were reënforced by three hundred cavalry from Fairfax, which made their force too formidable for us to cope with, and having one man wounded during the day (John Foster, of White Plains), Colonel Mosby ordered his men to be in readiness for subsequent emergencies, and to retire from the vicinity of Middleburg.

On the 24th, we were ordered to return to Loudon, and continue to collect the tithe, which was done under very great difficulties. A great many, in fact most of the farmers who had teams, had run them across the Potomac into Maryland, to prevent us from taking their corn and bacon. In addition to collecting the tithe, squads of men had been detailed to destroy all the distilleries in the county. The proprietors of these institutions had been ordered by Mosby to stop distilling the grain of the country; but no attention was paid to his orders. These houses had been broken up, and the stills cut to pieces in Fauquier, and Mosby was determined to terminate their traffic in Loudon. In addition to the injury the operations of these institutions would have on his men, they were consuming the very life-blood of the people. The principal one in Loudon County was Downey's, the proprietor of which was President of the Virginia Senate, under the Pierpont dynasty. He had fled to Maryland, and only returned when his property was occupied by the enemy His absence, however, did not interfere in the least degree with the distilling of grain. It was carried on as successfully by his wife as if he had been present. It was a rendezvous for the enemy, and had become an intolerable nuisance. A detachment of men were sent there by Mosby; and the stills were cut to pieces, and the liquor poured into the creek. Mrs. Downey determined to have her revenge. She had secreted in her house a squad of the enemy; and when Captain James, our Quartermaster, Major Hibbs, and John Bolling went to Downey's a few days after the destruction of the concern, to collect the tithe of bacon, they were, while dismounted, and in the house, seized by the enemy and carried prisoners across the Potomac River to Berlin, Maryland. Throughout Loudon County there was a general rejoicing when this nuisance was abated, and deep regret expressed at the capture of their benefactors.

CHAPTER XXXIX.

NEWS OF THE FALL OF RICHMOND—ORGANIZATION OF A NEW COMPANY—EXPLOIT OF CAPTAIN BAYLOR.

ON the 31st of March, Mosby surprised his men in Leesburg. While they were enjoying the society of the charming ladies of this place, he dashed in and ordered all of them to Carter's Mill, to do picket duty.

On the 2d of April, a meeting was held at the Quaker Church but nothing was done worthy of record.

On the afternoon of the 4th of April, heavy firing was heard on the other side of the river in Maryland. At dark, reports said, "It is in honor of the fall of Richmond." No credit was attached to it by our men. That night there was a great deal of speculation about it. The reports of those guns sounded like the death-knell to all our hopes and aspirations. We retired that night to awake in the morning and find it a fearful reality. The Baltimore papers received that evening revealed the fact to us. The intelligence produced great rejoicing among the loyal men of Loudon. Mosby and his men, however, did not despair, or give up the cause. A meeting was forthwith called (the 5th of April), at North Fork, at which there was a full attendance of the men. Mosby was much concerned about the news. In conversation with Sergeant Corbin and myself, he said, "*There is nothing else for me to do but to fight on.*" The men declared they would stand by him. A new Company was organized, and George Baylor, of Charlestown, Virginia, was elected Captain, Ed. Thompson First Lieutenant, Jim Wilcher Second Lieutenant, and Henry Carter Third Lieutenant; all elected for meritorious conduct.

Captain Baylor was a Lieutenant in the regular army, and had distinguished himself on many a battle-field, although a mere youth. By his daring and heroic conduct he had won the confidence and esteem of Lee, Stuart, and Hampton. As a successful scout he had no superior in the army, and on all important and hazardous expeditions, Stuart and Hampton called on him to execute them; and he did it successfully. His fame was not confined to our own army, but extended to that of the enemy. The foe in the Valley dreaded him as much as they did our own Chieftain, Mosby. Mosby had been for a long time anxious to have Baylor attached to his command. There was no way he could be had without promoting him to a Captaincy. He was already a First Lieutenant in the regular army, and if he resigned was liable to conscription. So this company was organized especially for him; and how worthy did he prove himself to lead brave men into battle! His first foray on the enemy will attest that.

After the election of officers and appointment of non-commissioned officers, Mosby told Baylor to go out and see what he could do. Baylor ordered his men (fifty), "to fall in," and moved off, with the best wishes of Mosby and the other men. The command was then ordered to return to Fauquier, and await further orders. Baylor passed through Snicker's Gap, thence down the Shenandoah River to Rock Ford, when he swam the river, under cover of night, pushed on down the Valley, and stormed Bolivar Heights at Harper's Ferry before day, capturing seventy-seven horses and forty-seven prisoners, belonging to Keyes' Loudon Cavalry, without a man of his receiving an injury. Captain Baylor, in this affair, annihilated Keyes, leaving him not a man or a horse; and had Keyes been there, he would have gone up too.

CHAPTER XL.

GLOOM PRODUCED BY THE FALL OF RICHMOND — MOSBY CONTINUES IN THE FIELD — BAYLOR'S UNWILLING RETREAT — ATTEMPT TO CAPTURE SCHOONERS — MOSBY INVITED TO SURRENDER — SOLDIERLY CONDUCT OF FEDERAL OFFICERS.

IT may prove interesting to the searcher after truth, to speak somewhat more in detail of our operations subsequent to the fall of Richmond. Gloom and despondency seemed to hang over the spirits of the people like a pall, notwithstanding the stout heart of our brave leader indulged the last ray of hope that we might yet be free, — that some stone would be cut from the mountain that could roll and carve the road to liberty. Mosby was not a guerilla; the tongue of calumny had made him such. He fought for liberty and independence, and conducted his campaigns not after the fashion of *Don Antonio Espozy Mina*, but as a brave, humane and Christian soldier.

On the 8th of April, the command made a rendezvous at Upperville. Mosby ordered Companies D and H to operate near Fairfax, and with Companies A and B repaired to the Valley, crossing the Blue Ridge at Ashby's Gap, and Shenandoah River at Ab. Ferguson's. After swimming the river, a halt was ordered near Ferguson's. Mosby took John Munson, Hifflebower, and Ed. Hurst, and dashed forth on a scouting expedition during the night and following day. In fact, the men went to work as though our star of destiny was unobscured by the clouds of adversity. John Russell, with seven men, captured and scattered the picket at Berryville, consisting of eight men with horses. Three of the men were killed, and three captured, two escaping, and of the horses seven were taken.

The next day, the 9th, Lieutenant Ab. Wrenn, took the detachment up the river, and bivouacked at Bethel Church, returning the following day to Ferguson's.

Mosby having returned, brought tidings of the capture of General Ewell, Custis, Lee, and others at Amelia Court House; but there remained yet a short time in which we could strike; and forthwith each detachment and squad lost no time. Twenty men, under Lieutenant Frank Turner, and twenty under Lieutenant Wrenn, were assigned to the Turnpike, between Berryville and Charlestown. Ed. Hurst went to Bunker Hill with ten men, while Mosby took Company A to Winchester, for the purpose of capturing a supply train from the enemy; but ascertaining that if he captured it (of which he seemed to entertain no doubt), it would be necessary to burn or destroy it, and thus lose the provender, &c., he declined to take it. Hurst and Turner returned without tangible results. Lieutenant Wrenn, however, under the auspices of an inferior guide, was carried into the meshes of the enemy's camp. Speed was then the essential atribute of a good soldier, and was called into requisition; for we fled with inconceivable rapidity. We did not debate the order of our flight, but *went* at once, and plunged across the old Shenandoah at Robinson's. Once safe across, we turned to behold the Yankees on the opposite side indulging in frantic demonstrations at our escape.

In this connection we must not neglect to

mention the exploits of the brave Baylor, in Fairfax County, and his portion of our command, who were busy (not as Beast Butler was at New Orleans), but whilst searching for *armed* enemies, were surprised and attacked in the rear by a large force of the Eighth Illinois Cavalry, under Captain Gibson. At the first fire Baylor's charger, which was a wild, unbroken animal, became wholly unmanageable, and went plunging into the woods and across ravines as though ten thousand demons from the lowest realms of perdition were in pursuit. In the skirmish Baylor lost two men killed and five or six captured, including Lieutenant Harney, whose loss was irretrievable.

The Second Squadron had been operating industriously on Northern Neck, under Captain Thomas Richards and Colonel Chapman; and whilst there, Richards embarked with several men in a frail scow, and attempted the capture of two schooners in the Bay. They were fired upon by a Yankee gunboat, and so closely pursued that the men were forced, as a *dernier resort*, to jump into the water and swim for dear life, until they reached the shore. It is needless to remark that our man-of-war fell into the hands of the enemy.

After gaining *terra firma*, the remainder of the detachment were collected together under Colonel Chapman, and during his efforts to procure arms for those who had been unfortunate in the Naval Expedition, word came that a detachment of Infantry, Artillery, and unbleached Yankee Cavalry, had been dispatched from Washington, with orders to show no quarter, but drive us into the Bay. Colonel Chapman resolved to fight it out, and as the shades of night approached made a charge upon them. In the melee Captain Samuel Chapman was severely wounded. The roads being in excellent travelling condition, the Yankees returned to Washington early next morning, and reported many daring adventures. Colonel Chapman's men then returned to Fauquier, not to engage in the approaching campaign, but to surrender, and lay down their arms.

On the 13th, a national salute was heard at Winchester, in honor of the Yankee successes and the downfall of our cause. As the sound of each discharge echoed and reverberated through the hills, it fell like the knell of departed glory upon the hearts of our people.

On the 14th, General Hancock dispatched a

ALFRED GLASCOCK.

courier to Mosby, inviting his surrender with comrades-in-arms, representing that General Lee, under whose command he was acting, had surrendered his whole army, and that surrender included Mosby and his command, giving a pledge, moreover, that his men should be paroled, and allowed to retain their side arms and horses, that were the private property of the men, but that Mosby himself would not be included in these terms. Mosby did not reply. A second courier came, offering and pledging to Mosby equal and fair terms with the balance of the army. Colonel Mosby was not a stranger to the studied and wanton vituperation of a mercenary press, and the malice and hatred cherished against him by the devotees of a senseless and degrading calumny. He concluded to delay an answer until he could communicate with his Government.

Alas! man's whole life is a tragedy, and here is the afterpiece. The last act in our drama had been played; the curtain was falling; we had no Government. Coercion was indeed a success, and whatever else might be our status, we were now conquered. The Government of our choice, which had flourished like a young giant, had been suffocated and crushed.

General Hancock's solicitude for the fate of our command was further developed by a proposition that an officer of equal rank with Mosby would be sent with orders to parole him, and Millwood designated as the point to consummate the business. Colonel Mosby lacked confidence, and postponed the matter. Colonel Chapman, Captain Thomas Richards, Adjutant William Mosby (brother to the Colonel), Lieutenant John Russell, and Surgeon Montero, visited, by special leave the headquarters of General Hancock, at Winchester. Each of these gentlemen will in after life recur to their kind reception and hospitable entertainment at the hands of General Hancock and his staff, with the most profound feelings of gratitude. Much anxiety and curiosity was manifested to see and converse with them, and they spent the whole Sabbath very pleasantly at the General's headquarters.

General Hancock revoked the order outlawing Colonel Mosby. A suspension of hostilities for ten days was agreed upon, and Colonel Mosby was allowed to confer with the authorities, fully, and learn the real desire of all good and brave men as to his future treatment. The lawless banditti, and cowardly, stay-at-home, white-cravat enemy, he knew would not entertain propositions for him to return to peaceful pursuits unmolested. He desired to know fully and fairly if the Government at Washington would receive his surrender in good faith as a finality, first to learn explicitly their terms, and then prepare to comply, and perform his part without reservation. There was an ominous Board of Military Justice, located in Washington, whose inquisitions were a novelty in modern civilization, and here was the rock on which many a poor unarmed Confederate, it was feared, would split. Their crimes were the more revolting because of their hypocritical pretence about *justice* and the public weal in their trials and semi-barbarous murders, their ex parte, manufactured, second-hand, newspaper evidence, their higher-law convictions, and their sanctimonious abuses of their victims, made it much more desirable with brave and honest men, to die with arms in their hands on the field of battle, than to be murdered by such a tribunal.

All the officers with whom Colonel Mosby conferred during the interim, were gentlemen, and who honored the uniform they wore, with great unanimity promised protection, but could not promise definitely, at that time, what would be the conduct toward him by this Board of Military Justice, so-called.

During the pendency of negotiations, the father of General Torbert visited headquarters at Winchester, and to gratify the earnest wish of the old gentleman, Colonel Mosby granted him an interview at Millwood. He expected to see a rough, uncouth demi-savage in the person and manners of Colonel Mosby, and was rather abashed when he was introduced to a Liliputian, physically, — one whose easy and unobtrusive bearing impressed his visitor of his rare qualities, his accomplishments, and gentlemanly deportment. Still the old gentleman seemed not to be able to overcome his prejudice and fears, and urged Mosby, with much earnestness and feeling, not to harm his son.

Mosby having failed to obtain reliable assurances from the Military Commission at Washington, at length ordered his whole command to meet him at Salem.

CHAPTER XLI.

MOSBY DISBANDS HIS FORCES AT SALEM — FAREWELL — MOSBY TAKES THE OATH — TEN THOUSAND DOLLAR PATRIOTISM — SUBMISSION OF MOSBY'S MEN — CONCLUDING REFLECTIONS.

THE men drawn up in line for the last time in the streets of Salem, calmly considered the fact that they must sever forever the cords which had so long bound their destinies in one common cause. It needed not the hand of the painter or poet to picture our emotions; they shone forth from every countenance, and spoke from every eye. The crisis had come; this ordeal could not be ignored; the trials of the war were severe, but this cup contained the concentrated bitterness of all our trials.

Adjutant William Mosby read to the command the following *farewell address:*

"HEADQUARTERS 43 VA. BAT. VOL. CAVALRY,
FAUQUIER CO. VA., April 21, 1865.

"SOLDIERS:

I have summoned you together for the last time. The vision we have cherished for a free and independent country has vanished, and that country is now the spoil of a conqueror. I disband your organization in preference to surrendering to our enemies. I am no longer your commander. After an association of more than two eventful years, I part from you with a just pride in the fame of your achievements, and a grateful recollection of your generous kindness to myself: and now, at this moment of bidding you a final adieu, accept the assurance of my unchanging confidence and regard. Farewell.

J. S. MOSBY."

The common sense and eloquent simplicity of this address, with the information it conveyed, was received by the men as the fond mother receives the announcement that her offspring has departed; its words were watched as we would watch and gaze upon the form of some dear one whose life was giving out its last ebbing pulsations; and then as each man grasped the honest hand of his brave leader, and pronounced the fatal word *farewell*, all eyes were moistened with tears of affection and sorrow. No one knew what was to be the fate of him who had just addressed us.

During the two succeeding days, Colonel Chapman and the greater portion of the officers and men visited Winchester, and were naturalized upon their native soil, and then returned to their respective homes.

Major Richards and Adjutant Mosby visited Amherst County on a mission of reconciliation and reconstruction. They there learned that General Joe Johnson had surrendered his command, and that the tide of war was rapidly flowing into peaceful channels.— Divested of all misgiving as to the final issue, they returned to Fauquier, and accepted the parole.

In the meantime, Colonel Mosby put himself in full communication with the Government at Washington, and undertook to comply with President Johnson's proclamation, if the Government would give him a quietus, and full receipt for all dues and demands, political, civil, military, and financial. The momentous question was decided in the affirmative, and the Government, after mature deliberation, accepted in a spirit of amity his proposition; and accordingly he returned to his allegiance by subscribing the prescribed oath. There were many men professing humanity and Christianity, and even styling themselves patriots par excellence, who thirsted for the blood of this noble man. Among such creatures, whose virus poisoned the atmosphere, were many persons who had never been injured or harmed by Mosby or his men; but they prayed for an opportunity to bathe their hands in his blood, and to take his life would have been esteemed a most refined luxury. Notwithstanding this fact was well known to the Virginia hero, after taking the oath, he laid aside his arms and visited Charlottesville, and other points, sometimes incog, and occasionally he made himself known to his former foes.

During a visit to the University, a Yankee accosted him, and asked him if he knew Mosby, the guerilla, and requesting him to describe the individual. He then dwelt with ecstasy upon the fact that a reward of ten thousand dollars had been offered for his capture, and wished to undertake the contract, and gain the reward. Mosby informed the *blood* speculator that he had seen the individual in question, but could not gratify him by giving him a reliable description. Mosby then mounted his horse, and went to Elijah Murray's house, about a mile distant. There he remained a few minutes, and departed for his father's in Amherst. He had scarcely got out of sight, when two hundred reward-hunters, calling themselves soldiers, dashed up to Murray's house and demanded Mosby as their prisoner. Their language on the occasion was not very select, nor by any means chaste, and the originality of their anathemas gave graphic evidences that they felt no personal risk in their undertaking. Every nook and corner was overhauled, and the out-houses, stables, negro quarters, sheds, &c., underwent a thorough search. These modern humanitarians, who, no doubt, had entertained numerous weak-minded dupes at church-meetings, with most heart rending accounts of the slave lash, and the brutalities of the "Slave Oligarchy," land pirates, horse thieves, &c., like Tam O'Shanter's wife, nursed their wrath to keep it warm, and were slightly enraged at the disappointment. A daughter of Mr. Murray, who was an invalid, had just entered the carriage at the side door, and was about departing for an evening drive, when several *patriots* rode up and shouted, "there's our game." The young lady, and the carriage, of course, had to be subjected to their GENTLE questions and searching gaze, and after an officer had removed her veil, the command retired with great eclat, in their usual good order.

When our hero reached his father's, he learned that General Gregg and Colonel Duncan, of the United States Army, had honored the family with a visit. They spoke of having a fighting acquaintance with Colonel Mosby, complimented him in very flattering terms, and expressed a warm desire to form his acquaintance. General Gregg, like a true patriot, soldier, and gentleman, offered old Mr. Mosby any protection he desired. On reaching home, Colonel Mosby expressed his gratitude at this manifestation of fraternal kindness, but he was forced by necessity, to forego the pleasure of returning the visit. At night he remained with a relative, William Hamilton Mosby, and during the day, spent most of his time at his father's.

During one of his first visits in this neighborhood after the surrender, the garrison at Lynchburg were advised, doubtless by some "*intelligent contraband*," that the brave cavalier was stopping with his father. Immediately an expedition of twenty-five men, led by a lieutenant, departed under the sable protection of night to win unfading laurels by his capture, albeit the moving cause was the ten thousand dollars, and visions of greenbacks danced through their heads. They reached a point within one mile of the house of Colonel Mosby's father, when a courier from General Gregg's headquarters overtook the party, with orders for their immediate return. They turned back, not however, without indulging in some trite phrases about "copperhead," traitor, rebel sympathizer, &c., &c. The demon of avarice continued to rage in the hearts of wicked men, and prowling bands were covertly scouring the country to such an extent, that General Gregg deemed it necessary to place a guard at the bridge across James River, with orders to allow no egress or ingress, unless the party held a pass, or his business was known.

Many incidents such as these go to make up the epilogue to the grand tragedy which had just been played. The acts of bad men sometimes served as a foil to set off the noble deeds of other men. Whilst Colonel Mosby now enjoys the seclusion of his home in Warrenton, Fauquier County, his grateful recollections of the kind services rendered him by the true soldiers of the Yankee army, will be cherished by him as the happiest emotions of his life.

The capture of Bolivar Heights, the action at Hamilton, and a few unimportant skirmishes, were the closing acts of the eventful scenes through which this hardy band had passed. Our boys, at the beginning of their campaign, did not have the glittering gems of wealth to lure them, nor the certainty of success to invite them onward; but actuated solely and honestly by inborn love for liberty, they bade adieu to the comforts and luxuries of home, and embarked their fortunes, honor, and lives in the sacred struggle for human freedom.

The capture of Richmond, the surrender of Generals Lee and Johnson, and the capture of our Chief Executive, thoroughly completed the work of subjugation. It then became our imperative duty, as faithful, humane, and honest soldiers, to contemplate the solemn task of coming under the yoke of the old Government, in a restored and unbroken Union of the States. Our men, not only as a body, but individually, at once turned their attention to the proper duties of good, law-abiding citizens. In proportion as each man had previously displayed activity and engaged in daring exploits for the "*lost cause*," he seemed to run to the opposite extreme, in adapting himself to the new order of things.

Mosby and his men never evinced the slightest vindictive feeling on the subject of reconstruction. They seemed willing, in good faith, to accept the arbitrament of the sword as deciding the issue against them. We speak for ourselves, as well as the command, that however much against our wish the tide of battle has turned, in common honesty and fairness we must adopt the axiom as true, "*once in the Union, always in the Union.*" Its truth has been sealed by the blood of nearly half a million brave hearts. The problem of disintegration and the establishment of two Governments with separate laws and distinct powers, has been definitely solved. Some of us contended that we were right, by virtue of an inherent right of revolution; others believed in the abstract right of secession; while another class denied the power or right of the general Government to coerce a sovereign State, and upon this theory took the Declaration of Independence as their magna charta; but whatever might be the ruling motives, all united to resist oppression from the dominant faction in the North. The primary issue of the war upon the part of our enemies was, " *the Union,*" *an unbroken Union;* and relying upon these professions, we were willing upon our surrender to recognize the hand of fate, frankly and honestly to acknowledge our mistake, that we had NOT been out of the Union during the four years of war, but that the Government of the United States is one, and must be as it was, minus the institution of slavery. It is a well settled fact, both in theory as well as practice, that the primary object of all just Governments under the ægis of civilization, is to impart the greatest amount of domestic tranquillity and happiness to the greatest number of people: we vainly indulged in the flattering belief that it was to be,

> " A union of hearts, a union of hands,
>   A union that no one can sever;
>   A union of lakes, a union of lands,
>   The American Union forever."

The axiom " that all just and free governments are founded in the consent of the governed," was finally ignored, when the last gun was fired, and with feelings of hope and confidence, we trusted in the magnanimity of a conquering foe. Speeches, proclamations, military orders, inaugural addresses, newspaper editorials, and private discussions with our prisoners during the struggle, had led us and the world to believe that the war was waged by the so-called Republican partisans, in good faith and honesty, to restore the Union and the dear old flag. In this we have been disappointed, as well as in our dreams of independence.

www.ingramcontent.com/pod-product-compliance
Lightning Source LLC
Chambersburg PA
CBHW032028220426
43664CB00006B/402